SPOOKY

Christmas

SPOOKY

Christmas

And Other Haunted Holidays

RETOLD BY S. E. SCHLOSSER

ILLUSTRATED BY PAUL G. HOFFMAN

**Globe
Pequot**

ESSEX, CONNECTICUT

Globe Pequot

An imprint of Globe Pequot, the trade division of
The Rowman & Littlefield Publishing Group, Inc.
4501 Forbes Blvd., Ste. 200
Lanham, MD 20706

www.rowman.com

Distributed by NATIONAL BOOK NETWORK

British Library Cataloguing in Publication Information available

Library of Congress Cataloging-in-Publication Data

Names: Schlosser, S. E., author. | Hoffman, Paul G., illustrator.
Title: Spooky Christmas : tales of hauntings, strange happenings, and other
   local lore / retold by S.E. Schlosser ; illustrated by Paul G. Hoffman.
Description: Essex, Connecticut : Globe Pequot, 2023. | Includes
   bibliographical references.
Identifiers: LCCN 2023009575 (print) | LCCN 2023009576 (ebook) |
ISBN
   9781493069880 (paperback) | ISBN 9781493069897 (epub)
Subjects: LCSH: Christmas--Folklore. | Christmas stories. | Ghost stories.
   | LCGFT: Ghost stories.
Classification: LCC GT4985 .S277 2023 (print) | LCC GT4985 (ebook) |
DDC
   394.2663--dc23/eng/20230508
LC record available at https://lccn.loc.gov/2023009575
LC ebook record available at https://lccn.loc.gov/2023009576

For Theo. Welcome to the family, little nephew.
Can't wait to watch you grow.

For Tim and Arlene. And for their children,
each of whom was born on/near a holiday.

For my family—David, Dena, Tim, Arlene, Hannah,
Seth, Theo, Emma, Nathan, Benjamin, Deb, Gabe,
Clare, Jack, Chris, Karen, and Davey.

For Greta Schmitz, Paul Hoffman, and the staff
at Globe Pequot. Thanks for all you do!

Contents

INTRODUCTION   ix

PART ONE: GHOST STORIES   1

1. *Cleves House*   2
    LIBERTY TOWNSHIP, OHIO

2. *Phantom Ahoy!*   10
    BALTIMORE, MARYLAND

3. *Ghost Skating*   17
    MANHATTAN, NEW YORK

4. *Christmas Guest*   24
    BUFFALO COUNTY, WISCONSIN

5. *Christmas Quilt*   33
    POY SIPPI, WISCONSIN

6. *Real Soon*   40
    LOS ANGELES, CALIFORNIA

7. *New Year's Goose*   46
    LONG ISLAND, NEW YORK

8. *Holiday Sleepover*   53
    DALLAS, TEXAS

9. *A Christmas Miracle*   60
    PALM BEACH, FLORIDA

10. *A Sprig of Mistletoe*   65
    BOSTON, MASSACHUSETTS

11. *The Blue Room*   72
    PROVIDENCE, RHODE ISLAND

12. *Find the Child*   84
    FAIRFIELD, NEW JERSEY

Contents

PART TWO: POWERS OF DARKNESS AND LIGHT   93

13.   *Der Belznickel*   94
ST. MARY'S COUNTY, MARYLAND

14   *The Christmas Dance*   102
DES MOINES, IOWA

15   *Chicken Thief*   110
SAN DIEGO, CALIFORNIA

16   *Baker's Dozen*   118
ALBANY, NEW YORK

17   *New Year's Hunting Trip*   125
MACKINAW CITY, MICHIGAN

18   *A Gift of Saint Nicholas*   141
MANHATTAN, NEW YORK

19   *Eavesdropper*   147
HAGERSTOWN, MARYLAND

20   *The Bachelor*   152
BEND, OREGON

21   *Wild Hunt*   165
LITTLETON, NEW HAMPSHIRE

22   *The Dollar*   176
BATON ROUGE, LOUISIANA

23   *Kobold Toymaker*   186
SHEBOYGAN COUNTY, WISCONSIN

24   *Gingerbread House*   194
BLOOMINGTON, MINNESOTA

25   *See My Gray Foot Dangle*   206
CHATTANOOGA, TENNESSEE

RESOURCES   227

ABOUT THE AUTHOR   233

ABOUT THE ILLUSTRATOR   233

Introduction

For some reason, this Christmas season was busier than usual. I always took an active role in the holiday season, participating in both the chancel choir and bell choir, teaching music in the Sunday School, attending holiday parties, and doing charity work. But this year was completely over-the-top. I had at least one activity scheduled for every single day of the month. It was insane!

By the third week in December, I was holiday-ed out and wanted to run away from it all. So, I took Friday afternoon off, had lunch at a nice restaurant, and then headed toward my favorite rambling spot at a local state park. Ringwood Manor was the preserved Revolutionary War estate of Surveyor General Robert Erskine. It featured a historic house with landscaped grounds, an old dairy building, a water wheel, a blacksmith shop, a large pond, and a trout stream. It was the perfect place to lose a few hours and regain my peace of mind.

As soon as I entered the long driveway, I realized something was up. There was a line of cars ahead of me. And I could see people queuing up in front of the lovely old manor house. What in the world? Then it hit me. It must be the final weekend of the Victorian Christmas open house. Every December, the manor was decorated from top to bottom by the local Women's Club, who charged an entry fee for visitors who wanted to tour the downstairs of the house. It was an annual fundraiser.

Well, this wasn't the quiet getaway I'd envisioned, but I'd always enjoyed the Christmas tours, so I parked in the lot and got in line to buy a ticket. The tour was self-guided, so I could linger as long as I wished in the intricately decorated rooms. And who knew? Maybe I'd chance upon one of the resident ghosts during my wanderings. Ghost stories were a popular part of Victorian Era Christmas traditions, so a ghost sighting would be appropriate under the circumstances.

I felt a chill pass over my skin as I stepped through the main door into the Great Hall with its herringbone parquet floors and grand staircase. Ornate paneling and arches gave a Gothic feel to the room, despite the many poinsettias, stars, snow houses, and evergreens that decorated it. The sixth sense I'd inherited from my Pennsylvania Dutch grandmother told me that an invisible someone was standing near the top of the staircase, watching the crowds and the costumed workers as they interacted in the hallway below.

I made my way through the Ryerson parlors, admiring the wreaths, candles, dolls, and ornaments. Evergreens decorated the mantelpiece above a Delft-tiled fireplace, and there were gifts under the tree. Then I entered the light-filled Glass Piazza, with its banks of poinsettias, sumptuous white Christmas tree, silver reindeer, and evergreen garlands. The drawing room overflowed with red and gold flowers, white candles, and fragrant wreaths. Lace Christmas trees, beaded garlands, icicles, and blue ribbons adorned the music room. And in the dining room, the massive table was set for a Christmas feast.

Everywhere I turned, there were the sights and smells of Christmas. I felt my body relax for the first time all season as I took it all in at my own pace. In the holiday hustle and bustle,

I'd almost forgotten what all the celebrating was for. Christmas was a time when light burst forth into the world to illuminate the darkness. It was a time when saints and spirits drew near to encourage generosity ("Baker's Dozen") and right wrongs ("Wild Hunt"). It was the season when good Saint Nicholas chained up the devil on the eve of his birthday—December 6— and made him visit the village children to see if they deserved the attention of *Kirstkindel* ("Der Belznickel").

And Christmas was the season when everyday people became heroes: like the stepmother who saved her stepdaughter's life when a troll threatened to steal her away ("See My Gray Foot Dangle") or the police detective who confronted a witch when children began vanishing from the Santa display at the mall ("Gingerbread House").

As I passed through the Great Hall on my way to the exit, I glanced up at the ghost, who still lurked on the staircase. We exchanged smiles, and I gave him a slight bow before leaving the house. I'd long ago made peace with the former owner of this haunted manor. It was his home long before the state laid claim to it, and I was honored whenever he took a moment to greet me personally.

The cold air of December brought color to my cheeks as I began my ramble through the Italian sunken garden before heading toward Sally's Pond. This afternoon was just what I needed to get back into the spirit of Christmas. Perhaps I'd drop by the family graveyard and see if the ghost of Robert Erskine was sitting on a gravestone or wandering the nearby gravel road carrying a blue lantern. It would make a great spooky story

PART ONE
Ghost Stories

1

Cleves House

When I mustered out of the military, I went back to my home state to settle down. I married my sweetheart and took a job in a town about ten miles from the place I was raised. Far enough away to have my own life, but close enough that we could visit my kin whenever we wished. Perfect.

Business drew me back to my old stomping grounds several times a year, and I always stopped to visit with my best friend, John Stow. John lived on a farm south of town, and his closest neighbor was a mean fellow named Cleves who'd spent time in the penitentiary during a misspent youth. Cleves was a penny-pincher who lived in a big old mansion that was run-down at the seams. He couldn't keep a housekeeper or handyman to save his life. Stories of his finicky ways and abusive language made good employees shy away, and even indifferent workers steered clear.

Cleves passed away not long after I mustered out, and his mansion was abandoned. He had no apparent heirs, and no one wanted the land. Folks claimed it was cursed. Carriages and horseback riders passing that way at night saw strange lights in the broken windows. One fellow claimed to hear moans,

CLEVES HOUSE

followed by a scream of terror so gruesome that it made his horse rear and bolt. The air on the grounds felt menacing; as if evil eyes watched every movement. Even the daring young men with young ladies to impress avoided the Cleves House. There were better ways to earn a smile.

It was a week before Christmas when I next came to my hometown. My carriage was filled with holiday presents for my parents and the Stow family, and I also had a very special Christmas present to pick up for my lady at the local jewelers. When this task was complete, John took me to the inn for dinner and then we went to the bar to have some very good brandy and swap holiday stories and jokes with some of the lads we'd known all our lives. It was late when we stepped outside to claim our horses, and snow was swirling all around.

"It will be a white Christmas," John said merrily as he carefully tucked an expensive bottle of brandy he'd purchased for his holiday feast into his saddle bag. We mounted and rode in the direction of the Stow home.

At first the snow fell lightly and talking was easy. Then the wind picked up and the snow grew thick. The ground was covered, and swirling snow made it difficult to see John's horse in front of me. My muffler iced up, and my eyelashes almost froze closed.

"John," I bellowed over the wind, hoping my friend would hear me. "We have to get out of this, or we will freeze to death."

"We are almost to the turnoff," John shouted back, stopping his horse. I could barely make out his figure just an arm's length away.

"The temperature is dropping too fast. The wind chill will kill us if we keep going. We have to find shelter, or the horses will drop dead of cold," I bellowed. "For God's sake man, if you want to be alive for Christmas, we have to stop now."

I'd been stuck in a storm like this once before, and only a roaring campfire built under an overhanging rock in the lee of the wind had saved the men in my brigade from an icy death.

"There's no place to go," John said. "Only the Cleves House." He gestured to the right, and I realized the looming dark shadow was the decrepit mansion. Out of all the local options, we ended up stranded in front of the haunted Cleves House. Fate was a fickle mistress.

"The Cleves House it is," I said firmly, grabbing John's reins from his shaking hands. I didn't know if it was the freezing air or fear that made him tremble, and I didn't have time to figure it out. We hadn't planned for a snowstorm. Our clothes were too light, and the wind was a killer.

I rode toward the looming darkness, trying to keep a straight path in the swirling blizzard. If we missed the building, we were dead. My horse gave a little jump and backed up a step or two. He'd hit his nose on the porch railing. I slid off and motioned for John to join me. Together, we coaxed the horses onto the porch and John threw the double doors wide so we could lead them indoors.

The shadowy mansion was festooned with cobwebs. The horses were uneasy being inside such a strange barn, but they didn't try to run. The house was freezing but at least we were out of the wind. We wouldn't make it through the night without a fire, so we started searching for something to burn. The front hallway was bare save for a massive cupboard and a fancy hat stand. But the parlor boasted several rotting couches and a broken card table with several chairs. We sacrificed the card table to the fire, and soon had a blaze going that warmed the parlor and made the front hall cozy enough to stable the horses there for the night. We divested them of their saddles and slung the bags into the parlor by the rotting couches. I found a bucket in the kitchen and melted snow for them to drink. Then we sat on the couches and lit our pipes.

"That was far too close for my liking," I said, studying John over my pipe. He was still trembling and had practically pulled the couch into the fireplace. I wasn't sure if it was the deadly cold or the supposed haunting that had him so rattled. To ease his mind, I started debunking the ghost stories we'd heard about the Cleves mansion as the killer wind blasted snow against the side of the house. My bravado didn't make a dent in John's pallor. His eyes kept straying to the shadows, and his thin hands continuously rubbed against one another.

A downdraft shook the whole house and the hall door creaked open. An icy wind swept through the room, making the flames burn blue and ghostly white, but they emitted no heat. "What the devil," I gasped, my body trembling with the sudden chill. "That last blast must have broken a window. We'll have to board it up quick or . . ."

I stopped abruptly, because John was pointing toward the door, speechless with terror. I turned in my seat and saw a skeleton looming in the dark entryway. Ye gods! I grabbed my gun and fired two bullets at the specter. The shots had no impact on the skeleton, but I heard the horses whinny and plunge in fear.

My military chaplain had spoken one memorable night about why ghosts haunt the earth. He taught us some phrases to use if we ever encountered one, and I uttered them now, desperately hoping it would work. "Speak foul specter," I intoned. "Tell us why you are here."

There was a rattling sound as the skeleton gathered itself. It advanced toward us, and I sat down abruptly beside my friend, still clutching my rifle. My heart was pounding harder than it ever had on the battlefield. The skeleton raised its arm. I thought it was going to hit me, so I raised my gun, reluctant to fire but not sure what else to do.

The ghost spoke. "I am dead," it howled in a voice that made the killer wind outside seem gentle and kind. "I am dead and yet I live a half-life that you mortals cannot understand!"

"W-who are you?" asked John. His voice was calm in spite of the tremors shaking his whole body.

"My name is Jamessss Symmmmms," the skeleton moaned. "I was robbed and killed in my sleep by John Cleves, who offered me shelter for the night." It pointed a bony finger to a ragged gap in its left temple. "He cut off my head and buried it under the hearth. Then he cast my body down the well."

As it spoke, the skull vanished from its shoulders. John yelped in surprise when the ghost's ethereal voice suddenly switched to the floor under the hearth. "Take up my head," it wailed.

One look at John told me he wasn't going to take up the skeleton's head. I grabbed my knife and started rooting around the base of the hearth. John took a shuddering breath and joined me, keeping as far away from the decapitated skeleton as he could. This struck me as funny, since we were digging for the poor man's skull. The hearthstones were loose, and we soon unearthed a fleshless skull with a gash in the left temple. I picked it up and it vanished instantly, reappearing on the shoulders of the hovering ghost.

"Thank you," the skeleton said. It seemed more alive now that it had its head.

"I have long wanted to tell someone my fate," the ghost resumed. "But none were brave enough to command me to speak. I have appeared to many, but you are the first to break my silence. If you please, give my bones a decent burial. And write to my relative, Gilmore Syms of Columbus, Georgia, to tell him what I have revealed to you."

The skeleton extended its hand. My stomach turned over, but I grasped it and shook. Its touch was colder than the killer wind. As cold as . . . well . . . the grave. It released me and I staggered backward and almost fell over John.

"I am at peace," the glowing skeleton said. It raised its right hand, and I saw that it was missing its pinky finger. A burning light surrounded the figure, growing stronger and stronger until I had to shield my eyes.

Then the light winked out and the ghost was gone. We were alone in the flickering firelight. Slowly, warmth returned to the room.

"Good God," John said at last. "I need a drink. I don't think we should save that bottle of brandy for Christmas."

"My friend," I said. "I agree."

We exhumed Syms's body after the storm and sent it to his cousin in Georgia to be given a decent burial, as requested by the ghost. When our task was complete, John vowed never to set foot on the Cleves property again.

"But the ghost is gone," I said as we took seats before the much cozier fire in the kitchen hearth at John's house while his wife bustled about getting us a hot drink and some food.

"You can't be sure of that," he said crisply. "Besides, *you* don't have to live next door to that foul mansion. Next time, I'll rather take my chances with the storm!"

2

Phantom Ahoy!

It was Christmas Eve about eight years ago when the ghost first appeared aboard our vessel. I was boatswain back then. My ship was sailing out of Baltimore, circling the globe looking for trade goods. The night was cold with a stiff breeze, and the sea was high. We had the royals and topgallant sails stowed, and all together it was a pretty wild ride.

It was after midnight. The watch had just been relieved, and Jim Barnet took over the wheel. None of us liked him much. He was a rum sort—a regular crank. The sailors were plenty nervous when he was around. Taylor was second mate in those days, and he had the watch.

We had a lot to cope with, riding those high seas. None of us were expecting it when Jim Barnet gave a mighty yell, grabbed a life buoy, and threw himself over the rail into the boiling waters below. I dropped the rope I was coiling, utterly shocked by what I'd seen. "Man overboard," I bellowed. Hard on my heels, Taylor gave shout to man the boats. We had the lashings cut in a jiffy and lowered the boats.

We swept the sea around our ship for nigh on four hours before we found Barnet. He had his arms through the life buoy

10

Phantom Ahoy!

and was completely senseless. At first, we thought he was dead, but the captain poured brandy into him while we rubbed life back into his cold limbs.

All at once, Jim reared up on the bed, looking as wild and frantic as he had at the wheel and shouted: "The ghost! The ghost! It's the devil. Take him away!" He kicked and shrieked and cursed and writhed like a madman. It took three of us to hold him down. He collapsed against the bedsheets in exhaustion a moment later.

I tell you what, folks, we were scared as anything. What had Jim Barnet seen up top that was so frightening he threw himself overboard? *Was* it a ghost? Or the devil? Were we sailing a doomed ship?

The captain was a religious chap and he scoffed at our fear. "He didn't see anything up top," he growled. "It was his conscience that got him in trouble tonight. God sent him a vision as punishment for getting drunk or gambling or something of that nature."

He dismissed most of the men crowding around, leaving just one of us to guard Barnet's bunk in case he came to and began railing again.

It was about 6:30 p.m. the next day—Christmas Day—when Barnet next awoke. Me and the mate were sitting next to him at the time. He grabbed me by the hand and cried: "Dick. Has he gone?"

I eyed him warily. I was pretty sure he was talking about the ghost. I replied soothingly: "Yes, he's gone, mate. We ain't seen him at all."

"Did ya check the mizzen? I see him now, up the mizzen. The devil! The devil's ghost." Jim's voice rose with each syllable until he was screaming. All hands in the forecastle had crowded around Barnet's bunk when they heard his voice. I heard the sailors murmuring to one another as Jim fell back on the bunk with a gasp. Sailors are a superstitious lot, and several men scurried to have a look up the mizzen.

They were back in a jiffy, and they looked nearly as scared as poor old Jim. The mate was shaking from head to toe as he exclaimed: "Dick, it's true. There's a ghost up there. You go look!"

"There ain't no such thing as ghosts," I said dismissively. But I knew the men wouldn't settle down until I took a look, so I went topside, expecting a practical joke. It wasn't a joke. The moon was full and illuminated the mizzen clearly. And right there, grinning down at me was a white figure with the face of the devil. I stood frozen, gazing up at the eerie sight until the captain strolled by and asked me what I was looking at.

"I'm looking at a ghost," I gasped through a tight throat and gestured upward.

The captain glared at the white figure and then glared at me. "Utter nonsense," he barked. "Can't you tell a practical joke when you see one? You go up one side and I'll go up the other and we'll catch our trickster, lickety split."

"I ain't going up there," I cried. My knees had turned to water at the sight of the devil ghost. I could barely stand, nonetheless climb. But Taylor the second mate was working nearby. He overheard the captain's order and volunteered to take my place.

So up they went, Taylor on one side and the captain on the other while I watched from below. The longer I watched, the more I became convinced of the ghostliness of the figure. Every time one of them drew level with the grinning devil, it vanished like smoke and appeared a moment later somewhere else in the rigging. They climbed up and down and across, trying to reach it, but never came near enough to make a grab for the phantom.

Finally, the captain came down, swearing worse than I'd ever heard him afore. "Call all hand, Mr. Taylor," he barked. "Let's see what rascal is up in the rigging. If I catch him, he'll regret it."

We mustered all hands on deck. All were accounted for, and yet above us we could still see the devil ghost grinning and pointing at us. The crew was terrified. The men wouldn't go aft to take the wheel that night, so the officers had to steer until the ghostly figure vanished from view.

It was a right pretty mess we had on our hands. The sailors were convinced we were on a doomed ship, and no swearing, lecturing, or direct orders would convince them otherwise. Still, the next evening the steward caught a glimpse of a white ghostlike figure vanishing out a porthole when he stepped into the pantry. A quick inventory showed the remains of the Christmas ham had vanished. "I don't think ghosts eat ham," the steward said. That got a chuckle from the men before the mast, and some of them returned to duties, although some of them thought it was the steward himself who ate the ham.

The ghost appeared in the mizzen again that night: up and down and all around the rigging, grinning its devil grin. The captain was furious. He tried to shoot the phantom, but every time he raised his six-shooter, the ghost danced about, vanishing from one place and appearing another.

"I've got an idea," Taylor said to me. "If the skipper can keep the ghost's attention on himself and the gun, I'll climb up the main and down the stays and drop a bag over his head. That should catch him."

"If he can be caught," I muttered. I didn't believe in ghosts, but that grinning devil face was making me doubt myself.

Taylor just laughed and we went to share the idea with our captain. He agreed at once.

For the next ten minutes, the captain and the ghost sparred with one another, guns waving, fingers pointing, swearing and dancing about. Meanwhile, Taylor climbed stealthily upward and then made his way to a spot just above the grinning ghost. He dropped the bag over its head and collared it.

"It's real," he shouted at once for the benefit of the watching crew. Then he swung and slid his way to the deck as the sailors cheered in the moonlight.

We crowded around and watched Taylor open the bag. A glistening white face blinked peacefully up at us. It was our monkey Jenny, covered head to toe with white paint with a gnawed hambone in her hand. The men exclaimed and laughed. I felt like a fool. Of course there were no such things as ghosts.

It only took a moment for us to realize that we'd been laying food and water out for her like clockwork, but no one had actually seen the little creature for several days. We reckoned Jenny must have fallen into our paint tub just before Christmas and had stayed aloft since then because she was too embarrassed to be seen.

The captain was so annoyed I thought he'd toss our pet overboard, so I gathered up the little creature and took her below to the little nest she'd made for herself. I briefly considered showing her to Jim but figured he wouldn't understand what he was seeing, and, worse, it might scare him further. Barnet babbled and thrashed and screamed every time he woke up.

In the long days that followed, it became evident that Jim Barnet had gone completely insane from his scare and the long hours spent in the cold sea. We were forced to leave him in an asylum when we docked at Cape Town. It was only at the end of our journey that we learned that Jim Barnet was an escaped convict sentenced for manslaughter. He'd mistaken the monkey for the ghost of his victim, and it drove him insane.

3

Ghost Skating

MANHATTAN, NEW YORK

I couldn't believe my luck when I got Melissa's phone number. We had met in early December at a birthday party in Yonkers, and I was amazed that this beautiful woman, who had the face of an angel, was still single. Melissa lived out in the suburbs, and for the first few dates, I drove out there to take her to dinner and the movies. Melissa didn't have a lot to say for herself, but she was beautiful, so I kept up my pursuit.

Melissa was an old-fashioned kind of girl. We didn't hold hands until our second date, and on the third, I was allowed to kiss her cheek. I was hankering to get my arm around her on our fourth date, so I plotted and schemed until I came up with a solution that should appeal to an old-fashioned girl. I would bring her to Manhattan and show her the Christmas lights and the amazing displays in the shop windows. Then we would go ice-skating in Central Park.

When I called her, Melissa seemed a bit reluctant, admitting frankly that she didn't know how to ice-skate. She was amenable to the idea though, until I mentioned coming into the city. You would have thought I had proposed trekking into the jungles of the Amazon. In Melissa's mind, Manhattan was populated with

17

GHOST SKATING

the worst sorts of criminals lying in wait for a sweet suburban woman to set foot upon its streets. At last, I got her to agree to meet me in the city, but she became so agitated about traveling from the bus station to my apartment building that I volunteered to meet her bus. This placated Melissa, and our conversation ended amiably.

On Saturday I waited patiently for the occupants of the bus to exit at Port Authority, hoping to spot Melissa before too long. I noticed a passenger whose heavy garb seemed to indicate that this was an explorer just arriving home from Antarctica. After further study, I realized the unusually dressed woman was actually Melissa, my date. It was a wonder she could move, muffled as she was from head to toe in so many layers of winter clothing. *At least she won't have to worry about muggers,* I thought cynically. *A bullet would never make it through all that clothing.*

I reluctantly went forward to claim my refugee from the Arctic and headed downstairs to grab a taxi. It was during this "dangerous" journey that I became aware of the advantages of bringing a suburban woman to the city. Melissa found it necessary to cling closely to me so that I could protect her from persons of evil intent like the lady selling flowers and the man sweeping the floors. As Melissa had not only the looks but the figure of a Greek goddess, her clinging was a rewarding experience.

Melissa was horrified when she learned we were to take a taxi to our destination. Apparently, riding in a New York City taxi was synonymous with death in Melissa's lexicon. I was prepared for this and kindly suggested that we take the subway. Melissa chose the cab. I'd decided that we'd start our Christmas adventure in Central Park and then walk around looking at the lights and displays before having a fancy dinner at my favorite restaurant. It was an excellent plan, if I do say so myself, and so I instructed the taxi driver to take us to the Wollman Ice Rink.

At one point in our ride, Melissa let out a shriek and nearly took off my nose pointing to a large object out the window. "What is that?" she cried.

"That's a horse," I said calmly, "and a carriage. Don't you have horses in the suburbs?"

Melissa bristled. "Of course," she said briskly, but there was a note of uncertainty in her voice, and I saw the taxi driver suppressing a smile. The horse looked a bit like my Uncle Hubert, but I didn't mention this to Melissa, feeling again that my sense of humor might be lost on her.

I paid the taxi driver and took Melissa over to the Wollman Ice Rink to rent ice skates. I had mentally rated Melissa's ice-skating potential as somewhere around a negative five (like her IQ, a wicked voice murmured in my head). I found that I had overestimated her ability. We wobbled around the ice a few times, with Melissa clinging to me so tightly that I nearly fell over. My arm was starting to go numb due to lack of circulation. *I should have taken her to a horror film*, I thought grimly. *That would have been a much easier way to get my arm around her.*

Suddenly, my eye was caught by a woman in an old-fashioned, long purple dress. She was skating figure-eights on the ice, laughing and obviously enjoying herself. I wondered why she was skating in costume. I didn't see any movie cameras around. She was joined by another woman similarly dressed in a green dress with a long, red velvet coat. They skated around and around, making figure-eights on the ice, obviously enjoying the lovely day. I felt quite envious, as Melissa and I plodded along at the edge of the ice. Melissa was whimpering unhappily to herself. Really, there was no pleasing this woman.

We turned the bend and found ourselves face to face with the woman in purple. With a quickening of my pulse, I realized that her feet were not touching the ice. And I could dimly make out the figures of other skaters right through her body. She was a ghost!

I must have gasped aloud, because Melissa looked up from the careful study of her feet and saw the woman skating toward us. We were on a collision course, and Melissa gave a small shriek as the woman skated right through our bodies. For a moment, all I could feel was an ice-cold mist moving through my frame. Then it was gone.

Melissa shrieked like a banshee, stumbled over her own feet, and we both toppled onto the ice. I rolled over quickly to gaze after the ghost. The woman in purple paused in the middle of her figure-eight to look at us lying on the ice. The woman in red stopped beside her, and they both laughed silently at the spectacle we made. Then they disappeared.

A crowd converged upon Melissa and me. We were picked up, dusted off, and a hysterical Melissa was helped over to the side of the rink. Somehow, I got her skates off and flagged down a cab to take us back to Port Authority, since Melissa refused to stay a moment longer in this terrible city with its muggers and ice-skating ghosts. I was feeling a bit shaky myself, but I was also annoyed that Melissa couldn't see how amazing it was that we had both seen two ghosts. Also, she had completely ruined my excellent date. I had dinner reservations at a five-star restaurant that had been very hard to obtain at short notice.

And we didn't get to look at the Christmas windows, which was one of my favorite holiday traditions.

I was in a very bad mood by the time I saw Melissa onto the bus. I walked over to Macy's to look at their window displays, but it just wasn't the same. So, I went home to eat takeout and watch a couple of my favorite Christmas films to soothe my bruised feelings.

Melissa called the next morning, apologized prettily, and invited me to have dinner with her family that evening. I was still feeling grumpy, but decided to give her one more chance, so I agreed.

In the afternoon, I went back to the ice rink to talk to some of the regulars. They weren't surprised that I had seen a ghost. Apparently, the lady in red and the lady in purple were sisters. Rosetta and Janet Van der Voort lived in Manhattan during the 1800s. They spent much of each winter ice-skating and loved to draw figure-eights on the ice. For Janet's thirty-fifth birthday, they threw a gala ice-skating party in Central Park with a feast spread on long tables and fireworks in the night sky. That evening, the sisters skated in the park with their friends, Janet wearing the purple velvet dress in which I had seen her, and Rosetta in a green dress with a red velvet coat. Both sisters had died in the 1880s, and their ghosts had been seen in Central Park since World War I. Usually, I was told, they appeared on the ice at night, but a few folks besides me had seen them in the late afternoon. I was fascinated. I spent the whole afternoon skating around the ice, hoping to see Rosetta and Janet again, but they didn't appear.

That evening, I drove to the suburbs to meet Melissa's family. I quickly discovered that Melissa was not the only family member to resemble a figure in Greek mythology. Her mother was a dead ringer, both in appearance and temperament, for Medusa, the Greek gorgon who had snakes for hair and a dreadful face, and whose gaze could turn men to stone. My father always told me that as women grew older, they started resembling their mothers. But surely Melissa would never become so grim-faced and bossy! Then I happened to catch a glimpse of her parents' wedding photo. I could see at once that Melissa looked exactly like the younger version of her mother. That decided it for me. I wasn't taking any chances. I made up a job offer in Australia, and that was the last I saw of Melissa.

But I am still hoping to see the ghosts one more time.

4

Christmas Guest

There! He heard it again. The soft thud-thud of muffled footsteps carried faintly through the midnight darkness and falling snow. Someone was following him.

He quickened his pace, pulse beating madly in his throat. He attempted a few surreptitious looks over his shoulder but saw nothing except swirling snow. But he could feel the other person's presence distinctly, and it made him nervous.

He moved quickly past the silent houses, aiming for his own home at the edge of town. His stride was as long as he could make it without turning it into a run. His mind was already racing. Why would someone follow him home from Christmas Eve service? Was it a thief, hoping he carried extra money in his wallet on this festive occasion? Or an unknown adversary? His pulse gave a painful throb at the thought, and he cursed himself for not carrying a weapon, or even a cane. But who thought of needing a weapon on Christmas?

He might be safe if he made it home ahead of his follower, though the house would be empty of all save his elderly housekeeper, sleeping in her small room on the top floor.

CHRISTMAS GUEST

Briefly, he regretted being an elderly bachelor who had never considered marriage. But that decision had been made long ago.

He was starting to tire as he turned into his street, fumbling under his cloak for the house key in his waistcoat pocket. His long fingers were trembling with cold though his body was sweating with strain, and his legs were hot and trembling from the unusual pace he was setting through the swirling snow. And then he realized that he could no longer hear footsteps behind him. He slowed his pace a fraction, listening hard, but there was only the soft frizzling sound of snowflakes hitting the houses and the streets.

Had his unknown follower managed to get in front of him, he wondered, picking up the pace again? Or had the footsteps just been those of a parishioner on his way home? The snow became heavier, driving against his face, his cloak. He had neglected to wear his hat this evening and regretted it now as he hurried up the stone steps leading to his front door. He turned the key in the lock and glanced back down the snow-filled street. There was nothing there, no footprints save his own. As the lock clicked open, he noticed that his arm was strangely free of snow. In fact, no snow clung to either hair or garments, though he had distinctly felt its coldness as it drove against him on the journey home.

Shaken by this strangeness, he leapt into the safety of his home and slammed the door shut against the memory of the frightening walk. But he couldn't block out the other odd circumstance. He touched his dry hair, where no hat had sat to shield it from the swirling snow. He touched his dry cloak, which should have been soaked through during the long walk through the storm. A single snowflake melted against his questing fingers and was gone. It was as if he had walked home in a bubble that had kept the falling snow away from him.

He was panting with superstitious fear as he took off the dry cloak and hung it on the coat rack by the door. Based on the condition of his clothes, one might be pardoned for thinking that he'd taken a stroll through a midsummer's night rather than a midwinter snowstorm.

A cold breeze seemed to sweep through the house, and he shivered and rubbed his arms as he mounted the staircase to the library. His housekeeper had kindled a fire for him before he left for the midnight service, and the room should be cozy and warm by now. He desperately needed the warmth after the strange occurrences of the past half-hour.

As he hurried into the library, a man's voice called his name. He blinked in astonishment, and then a huge smile lit his face. Sitting in a chair beside the blazing fire was Jake—the old friend and daring companion of his youth! Jake had long ago moved to Washington, DC, to take a position in the federal government, and the occasional letter was all he had heard of his friend during the years that followed the move. Yet now Jake was here, sitting in the old chair by the fire that he had always favored when he had visited in the past.

"Jake! What are you doing here, you old rascal?" he exclaimed.

The superstitious dread and apprehension he had felt during his strange walk home vanished unnoticed as Jake leapt to his feet in welcome. The two men shook hands vigorously and clapped one another on the back. He noticed that his friend's hands and body were icy cold, and he quickly urged Jake back to his seat by the fire.

"So you sweet-talked my housekeeper into letting you in, eh, old chum?" he asked jovially, not waiting for an answer. "What brings you home during this merry holiday season? I thought you were permanently ensconced in Washington."

"I had a yearning to spend one last holiday with my old friend," Jake said with a smile.

"And it's splendid that you're here! I was thinking on my way to midnight service that it would be a little lonely celebrating Christmas by myself," he said. "But come, tell me how things have been with you?"

Jake was glad to tell. The old men chattered back and forth merrily, interrupting each other again and again as one happy memory was jogged by another. He hadn't felt so elated in years as he did at this moment, sitting by the fireside with his old friend in the chair opposite him. Finally, he realized that he was being a poor host.

"Why, Jake, I've kept you here chatting and not even offered you food or drink!" he exclaimed. "Didn't my housekeeper give you anything? Never mind," he finished without waiting for his guest to respond. "I'll run to the kitchen and fetch us a snack. Want to come along?"

Jake shook his head. "I'll stay here by the warm fire," he replied. "Perhaps we can eat here? I'm still a bit chilled from my walk here this evening."

Remembering how cold his friend had felt when they shook hands, he nodded. He hurried to the kitchen and slapped together a cold supper, grabbing the first couple of plates he could find. They were mismatched—one with blue roses and one with yellow—but Jake wouldn't care. Then he poured a couple of tankards of ale and brought the whole kit and caboodle back to the fire.

They chatted merrily all through their late-night supper. It wasn't until he sat back in his chair, replete and contented, that his gaze fell upon the mantel clock, and he realized how late it was.

"Why Jake, I've kept you up half the night! How rude of me, when you've journeyed so far. Come, I'll put you in my best guest room, and we can chat again in the morning! My housekeeper makes an excellent breakfast, and Christmas dinner will be something to talk about for years to come!" He pulled his guest out of his chair and escorted him upstairs to the guest chambers.

"We'll talk more in the morning," he said again, as he showed his visitor upstairs. Jake smiled a little sadly and did not respond. He just stepped through the door and bade his host goodnight.

He returned to the master bedroom, which was on the same floor as the library. When he got to bed, he slept heavily but not well. He tossed and turned in his sleep, reliving the terrifying moments when he thought he was being followed home over and over again in his dreams. It was the sharp voice of his housekeeper announcing the imminent arrival of breakfast that finally pulled him from his bed, tousle-haired and red-eyed with fatigue.

"I'd better wake Jake," he muttered sleepily, pulling on his dressing gown inside out and putting each of his slippers on the opposite foot. After nearly tripping himself, he put his slippers on the correct way and struggled with the sash of his robe as he headed for the stairs toward the guest room. He'd just discovered that the sash was inside out because his robe was inside out when he caught a glimpse of the scene inside the library on the way past the door.

He stopped abruptly in astonishment. There, on the table where he'd left them, were the plates and cups they'd used the night before; but one plate was still heaped with drying, cold food, and one cup was full of untouched ale. He walked slowly into the study, staring at the untouched plate. It had yellow roses around the edges: the plate Jake had used. He'd seen Jake eating off that very plate last night around two o'clock in the morning and drinking ale from the mug beside it. He'd seen Jake putting the empty plate on the table right where it was sitting now. *Hadn't he?*

Turning on his heel, he raced through the door and upstairs, the ends of his untied robe flapping about like a shroud in a high wind. He knocked briskly on the guest room door and then entered without waiting for a reply. "Breakfast, old man," he said in a forced-jolly tone. The room was empty, the bed smooth and covered with a light sheen of dust. Obviously, no one had slept in this room for months.

"Jake must have been upset about the service after all," he said uncertainly, staring blankly into the empty room. "I hope he didn't stomp off in a rage. Or perhaps he was ill?" The knot in the pit of his stomach that had formed at the sight of the untouched food grew larger.

Ignoring his suddenly shivering body and the chills running up and down his spine, he ran downstairs to the kitchen and asked his housekeeper if she'd seen Jake that morning. The housekeeper's answer was short and to the point. She'd neither seen nor heard anyone arrive last night, nor anyone leave this morning. And she'd not stepped one toe inside the guest room. If there were to be two to breakfast, she wished her employer would see fit to tell her so immediately. If not, then she'd thank her employer if he would get out of the kitchen and let her finish her work. He backed out of the kitchen apologetically, saying that there would be "just one for breakfast" after all.

He stood in the hallway nervously trying to thrust his hands into the inside-out pockets of his robe. Why had Jake left without saying goodbye? Why was the plate with yellow roses still heaped with food? *Why had Jake bothered coming at all?*

The mystery disturbed him, and he spent a restless Christmas Day wandering about the house, picking things up and putting them down again absently as he tried to understand what had happened the previous night. He nearly terminally insulted his housekeeper by picking absently at his most excellent Christmas dinner, and he finally fell asleep in the library in the chair that his old friend had—or hadn't—occupied last night.

He awoke late the next morning, his neck stiff and sore from lying in the chair, to the sound of the front door briskly closing. He rose and tried to stretch out the kinks in his body, then headed out the door toward the stairs. His housekeeper met him at the top step with the morning mail on a silver tray.

"Here are your letters, sir," she said, handing the mail to him. She tutted disapprovingly when she saw his rumpled, slept-in clothes. "I'll get your breakfast," she said briskly.

He hardly noticed her departure as he glanced through the letters in his hand: a bill, an advertising circular, and a letter in an unknown handwriting. He opened the letter first. It was from Jake's daughter in Washington, DC. Her message was short and to the point: "It is with great regret that our family

5

Christmas Quilt

My girlfriend's mother has a pretty solid head on her shoulders, but when she told me her family owned a haunted quilt, I had a hard time keeping a straight face.

"I'm telling you, the quilt is haunted," her mom said. I glanced skeptically at my girlfriend, but she was nodding enthusiastically.

"She's not making it up," my girlfriend told me. "She once spent hours playing tug of war with a phantom. It kept jerking the end of the quilt, trying to pull it off her bed."

"It kept saying: 'Give me my Christmas quilt!' And then something would tug on the quilt," my girlfriend's mom confirmed. "Gave me quite the scare, the first time it happened. I had to hold tight to my end of the quilt to keep it from sliding off the bed. I didn't get a wink of sleep that night."

My girlfriend's mom spoke lightly, but her hands were trembling, and I realized she was serious. She really believed her family's quilt was haunted. More than that, underneath it all, I think she was afraid.

"Is it a new quilt? Something your family just bought?" I asked, settling into a kitchen chair beside my girlfriend.

CHRISTMAS QUILT

"Oh no. My parents found it when they moved into the house. It was in an old box in the closet. It's a lovely old quilt: a red, yellow, and black patchwork. It must be sixty or seventy years old. With one thing and another, they never got around to using it until I went to stay with them. When they put it on the guest room bed that night, it triggered the haunting," my girlfriend's mom explained.

My girlfriend took over the story then. The next person to sleep under the quilt was her aunt. When the phantom tugging started just after midnight, the quilt had heated up so alarmingly that her aunt had flung it from the bed. Her cousins had investigated the quilt. One of them felt a heartbeat when holding the quilt. Another had wrapped the quilt around himself while napping on the living room couch, and the quilt had whipped itself off his body and floated away.

My girlfriend volunteered to show me the quilt, which resided at her grandparents' house. After all the spooky tales about it, how could I resist?

After greeting her grandparents, we went up to the guest bedroom to look at the quilt, which was kind of pretty. Someone had obviously put a lot of time into its making. But it didn't seem the least bit spooky to me, and I examined it from top to bottom. No signature panel. No dedication to a long-passed loved one. No hidden skulls in the seams. Obviously, there was nothing to worry about here.

What did bother me was the look on my girlfriend's face when she touched the quilt. It gave me a funny ache in my chest to realize she was scared of this simple blanket. Impulsively, I said: "Why don't I take the quilt and put it on my bed tonight. Let's see what happens."

My girlfriend loved the idea, and her grandparents were eager to see how the quilt would behave in a different environment. The so-called haunted quilt was carefully folded into the old box and entrusted to the back seat of my old car. Then we spent the rest of our visit discussing all of the spooky quilt encounters to date and eating chocolate chip cookies with milk.

When I got home, I carried the quilt straight upstairs and put it on my bed. One good night's sleep under the quilt would prove the point, one way or another. I was eager to try it out. I didn't believe in ghosts, but who could resist such a story?

My mother came upstairs and cooed over the quilt. I'd never seen her so enthusiastic over a simple bedspread.

"It's handmade. No machine stitching at all. It must be very old," she said excitedly.

"And very haunted," I said dryly.

Mom ignored me. "You have to take good care of this quilt," she said sternly. "It was really very kind of them to loan it to you for your experiment."

"I will be a very careful ghost buster," I told her. "One way or another, the quilt goes back to them tomorrow."

Mom shook her head over my nonsense and then told me she and Dad would be away for the weekend. After a long list of chores and an even longer list of what I was not allowed to do while they were away (throw a party), she kissed me and went to pack their bags.

My folks left right after dinner. I spent a quiet, rainy evening reading a book before I went to bed. As I made myself comfortable, the door to the room creaked open. For a moment I had the strange impression that someone had come into the room.

I strained my ears, listening for a ghostly voice. I heard nothing.

I shivered and pulled the quilt up to my chin. Was it just me, or had the temperature in the room dropped several degrees? I could almost picture someone hovering on the ceiling, glaring down at me. I glared back into the darkness above my little cocoon of blankets but could see nothing.

Finally, I hunkered deeper into the mattress and decided I was imagining things. I turned over and forced myself to fall asleep.

Around midnight, I jerked awake, certain I'd heard a voice in my room. Was it the ghost? Suddenly, someone started tugging at the quilt on my bed. Instinctively, I clutched at the quilt and tugged back.

"Stop it," I cried, pulling back so fiercely that the muscles in my arms corded with the strain. The pressure released suddenly, and I fell back on the pillow.

I lay there with my heart pounding, and I swear that I *felt* the invisible presence step away from the bed.

Nothing else happened, so I tried to go back to sleep. But I was too keyed up by my ghostly encounter. I rose, intending to get a drink of water from the bathroom. Then I caught a movement from the corner of my eye and turned to see the quilt straightening itself out on the bed! I was all-over goosebumps as I hurried to the bathroom.

A moment later, someone pounded on the front door. I gasped. I knew, in the heart-wrenching way that all gut truths make themselves known, that the quilt phantom was at my front door. I thought about hiding under my parents' bed, but then I remembered the look on my girlfriend's face when she touched the haunted quilt, and the memory propelled me down the steps. One way or another, I was going to confront this phantom and make sure it wouldn't hurt my girl.

My skin was beading with cold sweat as I crept through the hall to the door. Every hair on my body stood on end. It is very hard to answer a door when you know a ghost is on the other side. I'd always scoffed at stories where the hero claims his knees are knocking. But—honest to goodness—my knees were knocking as I grabbed the knob with shaking fingers and opened it wide.

A dark figure loomed over me, glowing faintly against the heavy curtain of rain. It was shaped like a man, and the first thing I noticed was the figure was completely dry, which was impossible given the downpour outside. Then my gaze traveled upward, and I realized that *the man had no face.* The shock of it reeled me back on my heels. I screamed and my body shook with chills, my stomach roiled, and my chest was so tight I couldn't breathe.

After an eternity—or was it a single moment—the dark figure turned and faded away.

I flopped to the floor, gasping for breath. I had never been more terrified in my life. But I had to see this thing through. I ducked out into the rain and examined the muddy walkway. There were no footprints there or on the porch. And no other sign of my midnight visitor.

I went back into the house and my foot stepped on something soft in the dark hallway. I peered curiously down at the floor, wondering what it was. Then I shrieked in fear and kicked it away as if it were a poisonous snake. The Christmas quilt had followed me downstairs, trying to reach its former owner.

I confess, I raced upstairs to my parents' room and cowered under their bed until morning. Then I bundled up the haunted quilt and delivered it back to my girlfriend's grandparents with an abbreviated version of my ghostly encounter.

I have no idea what they did with the Christmas quilt after that. I never asked.

6

Real Soon

We knew right from the start that Johnny was going to be a soldier. Even as a child, all his concentration was on the military. So, we weren't surprised when he joined the Marines right out of high school.

Johnny excelled in his chosen career. He was so happy to be serving his country. I could see it in his face every time he came home on leave. He was itching to get into some "real action," something that—as a mother—frightened me. He was my only son, and I didn't want to lose him. But he was also a grown man with a wife and a baby on the way. I was very proud of the way he was living his life.

Then came the terrible day on September 11 when everything in our world changed. I knew as soon as I saw events unfolding on the television that Johnny was going to get the action he craved. And I started praying: "Please God, keep him safe."

Johnny went to the Middle East, and I started sending weekly care packages and checking my email several times a day. The tone of his communications was always cheerful, if a little strained. He was in danger many times, but somehow, he always

40

REAL SOON

made it through unscathed, although he lost a few friends along the way. This deepened him, and I saw a new maturity in my son that made an already proud mother even prouder.

My relief was intense when Johnny came home. I ran to him and almost knocked him over in my excitement when he stepped out of the car. He hugged me tightly, and then reached into the backseat to remove his little daughter from her car seat and show her off to us.

I tried to conceal my fear when he told us a few months later that he would be going back to the Middle East. But Johnny knew me pretty well. On his last leave before deployment, he took my hand, kissed me on the cheek, and said: "I love you, Mom. We'll be together again real soon." I held back the tears until he was gone. Then I wept like a child.

Johnny's emails on this trip were sporadic and his tone was grim. Things were tough over there, although he did not say much about it. He just spoke of little things like the rapid growth of his beautiful girl and the many activities of the wonderful woman who was her mother and his wife. After he'd been gone nearly a year, Johnny started making plans for his return home. He thought he might make it home in time to celebrate Hanukkah with the family, and I clung to that hope with all my strength. My husband and I had always made a big fuss over Hanukkah, ever since Johnny was a little boy. The eight-day Festival of Lights commemorates the re-dedication of the Temple in Jerusalem after its desecration by the forces of Antiochus IV and celebrates the "miracle of the container of oil." According to the Talmud, at the re-dedication following the victory of the Maccabees over the Seleucid Empire, there was only enough consecrated olive oil to fuel the eternal flame in the

Temple for one day. Miraculously, the oil burned for eight days, which was exactly the length of time it took to press, prepare, and consecrate fresh olive oil. Since that time, the Jewish people have celebrated both victory and miracle each year by kindling the lights of a special candelabrum, the menorah or hanukkiah, one light on each night of the holiday, progressing to eight on the final night. We read the sacred story, pray special prayers, eat latkes and fruit-filled donuts, play games with our children, and give gifts. It is a time of great joy for our family.

When Johnny emailed us the news that it looked like his tour would be extended, I was upset. I had my heart set on us being together for Hanukkah this year, and the news hit me hard. But I kept on smiling, proud of my soldier boy, and only cried once when no one was around. We had my daughter-in-law and granddaughter over on the first night of Hanukkah and showered them both with food and gifts. If, perhaps, we acted a little too happy, a little too cheerful, well, who could blame us? We were all keenly aware of the beloved one who was missing from the occasion.

Late that night, I awoke from a deep sleep, certain that I had heard Johnny's voice. "Mom," Johnny said again. I turned over and blinked in the dim light coming from the streetlamp outside our window. Johnny was standing beside the bed, gazing down on me tenderly. I sat up immediately, my heart beating faster in excitement. Johnny was back. He had come home for Hanukkah after all! They must have decided against the tour extension.

"Johnny," I gasped.

He smiled and sat down beside me, as he had often done when he was little. He took my hand and said: "I want you to know how much I appreciate you and Dad. It couldn't have been easy, raising a headstrong boy like me, but you did a wonderful job."

Johnny's words filled me with a great joy and a terrible fear. The military had sent him home, hadn't they? (Hadn't they?!?) Something in his beloved face told me that this was not an ordinary visit. That he hadn't come home the normal way. My heart thundered in my chest, and I began to tremble, dread making my limbs feel heavy. Tears sprang to my eyes, and Johnny gently wiped one away with his finger. "I came to tell you that I am all right," he said quietly. "Take care of my girls for me."

"We will," I managed to say, realizing at last what this visit meant.

"I love you, Mom. We'll be together again real soon," Johnny said. He leaned forward, kissed me on the cheek, and then he was gone.

I fell back against the pillows, too stunned even to weep. My husband, who was a heavy sleeper, woke when he felt the bed jerk. He rolled over and mumbled: "Are you all right?"

"Something has happened to Johnny," I said, too grief-stricken to be tactful. "I think he's dead."

My husband jerked awake. "What?!" he exclaimed fearfully. I started sobbing then and told him about Johnny's visit. We held each other close for the rest of that long night, waiting for dawn and the news which would surely come with it.

The days following the official notification of Johnny's death—killed in action in the Middle East—were mind-numbing. I clung to the words my boy had spoken to me in the moments right after he died. Johnny had said he was all right, and I believed him. My son's body was gone, but his essence, his soul, everything that made him my Johnny was safe and well. And we would be together again real soon.

7

New Year's Goose

If ever a man was henpecked, that man was Nicholas van Wemple. He was a stout, round little fellow with a beaming smile and all the energy of a cat sleeping next to a good fire. He was quite well-to-do, but Mistress van Wemple held the purse strings, and she did not give him so much as one coin to spend on schnapps. Nicholas was rather hurt by this frugality, but he was too lazy to do anything about it. Mistress van Wemple had industry enough for three people, and she divided it equally between cleaning her house from top to bottom and scolding her phlegmatic husband in as shrill a tone as ever a hen used on her rooster.

Now around about Christmastime, a new rumor spread through town. Folks began saying the old mill was haunted. Mysterious lights would float around the mill in the middle of the night. Some men walking home from the tavern one evening had heard voices coming out of nowhere, and then they heard the terrible shrieking of a ghoul. It had scared them sober, so horrible was the cry. People started avoiding the mill after dark.

Mistress van Wemple scoffed at the stories of the supernatural and forbade Nicholas to talk to any of the men

New Year's Goose

who had heard the unearthly scream of the ghoul. "Drunkards, the lot of them," his good mistress screeched at him, waving a dust cloth under his nose and making him sneeze. "And you would spend all our money on schnapps, just like the rest of those good-for-nothings if I would let you, Nicholas!"

"Of course not, my dear," Nicholas lied with a beaming smile. Folks in town could never figure out what Nicholas saw in his wiry-haired, double-chinned, red-faced wife, but he was as enamored with her after twenty henpecked years of marriage as he was on the day they took their vows.

On New Year's Eve, Mistress van Wemple reluctantly counted out ten coins into her husband's hand and sent him to fetch a fat goose from Dr. Beck. "Do not stop at the tavern, Nicholas van Wemple," she screeched at him as he clapped on his hat and meandered out the door. "That money is for the goose, do you hear! Not for schnapps!"

Nicholas blew his bride a kiss and strolled down the icy road toward Dr. Beck's house, humming happily to himself. As he passed the tavern, a roguish breeze snatched his hat from his round head and blew it in the open door. Nicholas went to fetch his hat and was hailed at once by several of his friends. Smelling schnapps and tobacco, Nicholas beamed with delight and slid into a chair. *Now this was really something*, thought he, forgetting the goose entirely. He ordered up a schnapps, was treated to a second by his friends, and bought everyone a third round. As his pile of money disappeared into the till, his friends laughingly asked him what his wife thought of his night on the town. Nicholas grinned good-naturedly and said, "Well now, 'tis my money any way you look at it."

"That's not what my wife says," chuckled his next-door neighbor.

The warm bar and the schnapps were making Nicholas rather sleepy, so he laid his head down for a quick snooze. He woke with a start an hour later. His friends had all left the tavern, and the only voices he heard came from the next room. Two sailors with leather jackets, black beards, and earrings were talking together in low voices. Nicholas listened rather sleepily for a moment before he realized they were discussing some gold that had been buried in the cellar of the old mill. The two men finished their drinks hastily and hurried out of the tavern.

Nicholas left the bar slowly, his mind still in a haze from all the alcohol he had consumed. Only one thing was clear to him in his advanced state of inebriation: He had spent all his money on schnapps and had no goose to take home to his wife. *This is not a good thing*, he mused. He decided that he should visit the mill in hopes of retrieving the gold and fetching home the goose before his wife learned about his latest escapade at the tavern.

Sneaking into the shed behind his house, Nicholas found an old shovel and a lantern. Then he marched as fast as his stout body and fat legs would take him to the decrepit old mill. He hesitated for a moment when he saw the tumble-down building looming dark against the white snow, remembering the rumors of floating lights and unearthly shrieks. But the hope of gold urged him into the creaking darkness of the mill and down the wobbly stairs to the old cellar.

The earth of the cellar had not yet frozen, so it turned easily under Nicholas's shovel. Soon, the tip of the shovel hit something. Nicholas dug deeper and unearthed a canvas bag.

As he hauled the bag out of the hole, a seam ripped, and gold coins spilled all around him. This sudden wealth was beyond anything Nicholas had dreamed of! He began stuffing the legs of his breeches with coins, humming happily to himself and dreaming of the smile that would light the face of his good wife when she saw the gift he brought her.

The tread of feet on the rickety stairs brought Nicholas to his senses. He turned just in time to see four scruffy sailors enter the cellar. Two of them he recognized from the tavern. The other two were strangers. The men blinked in the lantern light, looking at the hole, at the open bag of gold coins, and lastly at Nicholas. He stared back, realizing suddenly that these were pirates. *So it is buccaneers who have been haunting the old mill*, he thought cheerfully, as they frog-marched him up the wobbly stairs, gold coins spilling out the bottom of his trousers with each step.

The pirates sat Nicholas down unceremoniously next to the small fire they had lit, pushed a glass of hot cider into his hands, and forced him to drink a toast to their pirate flag. As a general rule, Nicholas did not approve of pirating as a profession, but pirating that involved hot cider couldn't be all that bad, to his way of thinking. He cheerfully downed his drink in one gulp and then gave a shout of surprise when two of the pirates grabbed his stout, round form and pitched him out the window. Nicholas grabbed desperately at a bundle hanging from the window frame as he sailed through, trying to save himself. The frayed rope holding the round object broke, and Nicholas had just enough time to realize he was clutching a goose that the pirates had stolen from a neighboring farm before he landed in the water and the mud outside the mill.

Nicholas kicked his way to the surface of the pool, jumped out of the mud as fast as he could, and staggered through the ice and snow in the general direction of his home, clutching the goose to his chest as he ran. He was nearly home when the events of the evening, coupled with the hot cider and the schnapps, overwhelmed him and he fainted into a snowbank a few feet from his door.

He was awakened in the wee hours by the shrill tones of Mistress van Wemple, who had discovered him missing from their bed and had hurried to look for him. He gazed blurrily up into her rough, beloved face and wordlessly thrust the featherless goose into her arms. Mollified by this unexpected gesture, Mistress van Wemple hurried her husband into the house, pulling off his snow-covered garments and forcing him into warm, dry nightclothes. She even heated up some cider she had hidden away from him and put his feet into a hot-water bath before she demanded to know where he had been all this while.

Nicholas eagerly told his tale of schnapps, gold, pirates, and the goose. Mistress van Wemple did not believe a word of it. There had not been one gold coin in his britches when she had removed them, nor any in his boots!

"You are drunk, old man," she scolded, kissing him on the forehead.

"If I am drunk, old woman, then how could I afford to bring you a goose?" asked Nicholas. "Ask any man at the tavern, and he will tell you I had not one coin on me when I left!"

"I still say you dreamed the whole thing," said Mistress van Wemple. "Now finish up your cider and come to bed."

Nicholas obediently drank his second cup of hot Hollands of the night and then followed his good wife up the stairs.

He told his story to their New Year's guests the next day while they partook of the roasted goose, but none of them believed him. After dinner, the men walked with Nicholas out to the old mill to check for the pirates, but the mill was empty and not one glimmer of gold was left on the creaking stairs or in the dirt of the cellar. Ever after, the story was told with many a wink and a laugh at Nicholas's drunken fancy. But Nicholas didn't care. He noticed that after his encounter with the pirates on New Year's Eve, the mysterious lights and voices vanished forever from the mill.

And it is all on account of van Wemple's goose, Nicholas chuckled to himself.

8

Holiday Sleepover

The whole extended family was together this year for Christmas—brothers, sisters, aunts, uncles, and cousins. There were a lot of us. We were all crowded into our grandparents' farmhouse and several RVs. Each of the adults—couples and singles—got their own rooms, but all the boy cousins and girl cousins had to share. Which wasn't too bad really. We thought of it as one big holiday sleepover.

There were four of us older girl cousins sharing a room on Christmas Eve—Sue, Jill, me, and, of course, May. We weren't too happy about having May with us. She had already graduated from college, and her whole life was focused on dating and getting married. She'd been boasting all week about how her boyfriend was going to propose to her sometime during the holidays. Her younger brother, Abe, wasn't so sure about that. He'd told us her boyfriend was getting ready to dump her. But May had the self-confidence of a princess and wouldn't have believed him even if he said anything. So, he kept mum.

It was May who'd started talking about holiday folk traditions when we retreated to our shared bedroom on Christmas Eve. We were too excited to sleep, so May started telling us about

HOLIDAY SLEEPOVER

the various ways you could scry the future on Christmas. One way was to walk naked around the central chimney at midnight to see the face of your future husband. That started us giggling.

"Too bad we don't have a central chimney," Jill giggled. "May could find out when her boyfriend will propose."

"If he will propose," muttered Sue.

May just laughed. "You are jealous," she accused from the soft comfy bed, which, of course, she'd appropriated since she was the eldest of the girl cousins. The rest of us were in sleeping bags on the floor.

"I've heard that animals speak on Christmas Eve," I said, citing another Christmas folktale to forestall a fight. "They tell secrets and list everyone who will die in their town in the coming year."

All of us looked at Sue's small Yorkshire terrier, who was snoozing at the foot of her sleeping bag. The small dog blinked at us but did not volunteer a comment, so that folktale probably wasn't true.

"I've heard that if you throw a shoe over your shoulder on Christmas Eve, it will tell you if you are going to get married," said Jill, returning to the original topic.

"How?" I asked skeptically.

"If the toe of the shoe points toward the door, you will get married. If it points inside the room, you won't. Oh, and if it points to one side or another, that means you are going to travel," Jill replied.

"Well, that's simple enough," said Sue. She grabbed a shoe from the pile of clothes beside her sleeping bag and tossed it over her shoulder toward the doorway. It landed with the toe facing the door. "That's me settled, then," she said cheerfully.

A moment later, three more shoes went flying toward the door. When everything had thudded satisfactorily to the carpet, we discovered that Jill and I were also going to get married, but May's shoe was facing inward.

Sue started laughing, but May was furious. "I am too getting married," she said forcefully. "Billy is going to propose. Probably tomorrow. You'll see. I'm driving to his house after lunch to exchange gifts. There will be a ring for me under the Christmas tree." But she didn't sound as certain as she had a moment ago.

"I've got some apples we can use to check," Jill called, rummaging in her snacks bag.

"Check with apples?" I asked skeptically. Really, who knew there were so many crazy folktales around Christmas foretelling? My cousins were obviously experts. Or possibly just insane.

"Sure. You cut open the apple down the middle, and if the seeds are in the shape of a cross, something bad will happen in the coming year. If they are in the shape of a star, something good will happen."

Jill tossed May an apple, then distributed the rest among us. We had a bit of a rough go cutting them down the center with the plastic knives from the snack bag, but when we were done, only three of us had stars. My stomach dropped when I saw May's apple. Twice in a row, the symbols pointed to disappointment for May. The others thought this was funny, but I had a funny knot in my middle. I didn't like that.

May glared at the cross in her apple. "That does it. What do I need to do to prove it to you?"

She jumped up from the bed and went rummaging in the closet, where our grandparents stored the board games, sporting goods, and toys. A moment later, she pulled out a Ouija board. I gulped. My parents didn't want us messing with the occult, so they'd told me plenty of cautionary tales about how dangerous Ouija boards were. But hey—it's just a game, I told myself as my cousin banged the board down in the center of the sleeping bags. Can't hurt anything, right?

It was a strange-looking board, covered with letters and symbols and the words "yes" and "no." There was a plastic pointer that was supposed to move across the board at the behest of the spirits. The instructions called it a planchette. The sight of the board made me nervous, but I put it down to the late hour and the scary reputation of the game.

It was almost midnight—the so-called witching hour. Christmas Day was only moments away when May began our little game. May and Jill put their fingers on the planchette, and May said briskly: "Is Billy going to propose today?"

At once, the planchette swooped over to "No."

"You did that on purpose," May growled, glaring at Jill.

"I did not," Jill protested. But May made her take her hand off the planchette.

"Ask it again," urged Sue.

"Is Billy going to propose today?" May asked. She tried to push the planchette toward yes. I could see the pressure in her fingers, but it refused to budge. As soon as she released the pressure, the planchette swept definitively toward the No.

"Let me do it," Sue said. She grabbed the planchette and said: "Is Billy going to propose to May today?"

The planchette moved to No.

"Tomorrow?" she ventured. The planchette stayed on No.

"Too specific," I said.

"Is Billy going to propose to May?" Jill called from her sleeping bag.

The planchette stayed on No.

May was furious. "You are all jealous of me," she cried, seizing the planchette from Sue.

"Am I going to get married this year?" she cried, pushing the planchette forcefully toward the yes. The planchette froze in her hand as if it had rooted itself to the Ouija board and refused to move.

Goosebumps crawled up my arms. I'd never seen anything like it. The planchette wouldn't budge.

"Tell me the future, you . . . stupid . . . thing . . ." May shouted, pushing with all her might on the last three words.

From somewhere behind Sue, a high-pitched voice said: "You have no future."

We froze in place, shocked by a foreign presence in our midst.

"What was that?" whispered Jill.

We all turned in the direction of the voice. No one else was in the room. Sue's small Yorkie, still lying on the end of the sleeping bag, cocked her head inquiringly, watching our antics. My stomach turned as I remembered the tradition of animals foretelling the future on Christmas. Had the little dog spoken?

"This is ridiculous," May said. "You are all jealous of me because I'm getting married, and you aren't even dating. I'm going to bed."

She threw the Ouija board at the wall. It toppled to the floor beside our shoes. The planchette came unstuck and slid over to the No. I gulped and glanced at my suddenly somber cousins. Sue and Jill looked from the Ouija board to the Yorkie and then dove into their sleeping bags. May stomped to the bed and pulled the covers over her head. Alrighty then. I slid off my sleeping bag and turned out the lights.

My thoughts whirled round and round, long after my cousins' breathing indicated they were asleep. But finally, I grew drowsy. Just before I fell into dreams, I thought I heard the high-pitched voice one more time: "You will get your scholarship this year, Lucy."

"Oh good," I mumbled and drifted off to sleep.

Christmas morning was the usual chaos of small children waking at 5:00 a.m., eager to look in their Christmas stockings. This was followed by a huge breakfast and then gift giving around the tree. Everyone was in a wonderful mood, the strangeness of the late-night Ouija session forgotten. Only May seemed discontented. Her brother Abe reckoned it was because Billy hadn't been invited to our morning gathering.

As soon as presents were done, May borrowed her parents' car and drove across town to see Billy and spend the afternoon with his family. About an hour and a half after she left, one of the cousins came running into the living room where we were watching Christmas movies and shouted that a police car had pulled into the driveway. The doorbell rang an instant later, and our grandfather went to the door. There was some discussion and shuffling around the front door, and then my aunt started to scream. Sue, Jill, and I leapt up from the couch and went running into the hall. My aunt was sobbing against her husband's shoulder and my grandfather was talking grimly to a police officer.

Abe turned to look at us, his face white with shock. "May was in a car accident. A semi slid on the ice and hit her car head on. She's dead." He sat down abruptly on the floor, unable to stand.

Through the shock and horror of that moment, I remembered the high-pitched voice speaking to May last night: "You have no future."

I looked frantically around the hallway and spotted Sue's small Yorkshire terrier standing in the doorway to the living room. We stared at one another for a long moment. Then the dog trotted behind the Christmas tree and disappeared from view.

9

A Christmas Miracle

PALM BEACH, FLORIDA

I was in Florida seeking a winter home to purchase as a Christmas gift for my beloved wife, when I suddenly took ill with a high fever. I am a physician by trade, and I will be the first to confess that doctors make the worst patients. I ignored my symptoms and continued to review properties, though my knees trembled, and I was increasingly overtaken with shivers.

By evening I had put myself in extreme danger. I tossed and turned for several hours, my fever rising perilously high. I was too weak to care for myself, and I had left my family at home in New York, so no one shared my hotel room and none of the other guests knew I was ill.

Around midnight, my whole body seized up and I lay in my hotel bed, paralyzed from head to toe. I realized that this was the end of me. In the morning, my dead body would be discovered by the hotel staff.

Suddenly, I found myself floating above the bed in spirit form, gazing down at my paralyzed body. It looked smaller, somehow, as if its significance had already waned. I thought of the sorrow my wife and children would experience when they

A CHRISTMAS MIRACLE

received the news. Then I pictured the grief of my best friend, who had moved to the West Coast the previous year.

In the instant I pictured my friend's face, I was transported across miles and found myself standing in a large sitting room next to a large Christmas tree. I recognized the place instantly as the California home of my best friend. I saw my friend and his wife seated around the fireplace with several other couples, laughing and chatting over holiday drinks and dessert. I clearly heard their banter, and I watched as my friend cracked a few jokes that convulsed the whole group. One of their small children came running into the room for a goodnight kiss and was lovingly scolded for staying up past her bedtime. My friend scooped up his daughter, placed a Santa hat on her curly head, and waltzed her around the room and out the door. I called his name as they danced past, but he didn't hear me.

While my friend put his little girl to bed, I tried to gain the attention of his wife, who was refreshing drinks and getting her guests second helpings of dessert. She too did not notice my presence, even when I stood right in front of her and waved my hands before her eyes.

My heart sank. I turned away from the merry group by the fire just as my friend returned to the room. He walked through the door, and we came face to face with each other. His jaw dropped in astonishment, and he called my name. "Jack! What are you doing here? I thought you were in Florida looking at houses!" He stepped forward with a glad smile, stretching out to shake my hand.

And suddenly I was back in my hotel room, staring down at my frozen body. How much time had passed? I wondered bleakly. As I hovered in that dark place, the air around me started to shimmer. Soon, my spirit was enveloped by a lovely bright light. Out of the glow, I heard a voice of such strength and beauty that it moved me to tears. "Do you have any work left to do?" The voice inquired. "Or would you like to come home?"

The sound of that voice made me long for my heavenly home. Then I thought of my wife and children, of my best friend, of my many patients and all the projects I had left unfinished. "I think I need to go back," I said. "At least for now."

"Then you may return to earth," the voice said.

The light vanished, and I found myself back in the hotel room, hovering over my body. I willed myself heavier and my spirit form slowly descended until it was right on top of my physical form. I clenched my fists and chanted: "Lower, go lower. You must reinhabit the body."

I don't know how long the mental struggle lasted. It felt like forever. Then I felt some kind of physical barrier give way, and I inhabited my body once more. My eyes opened with a snap. My whole frame convulsed, and I gave a great gasp, hauling air into my lungs and shaking from head to toe. I brushed my hand over my face and realized I was covered with sweat. My fever had broken, and I would live. I saw the light of dawn spilling through the curtains of my hotel room and knew I had spent the greater part of the night out of my body. My recovery was a Christmas miracle. I buried my face in the pillow and thanked the good Lord for his mercy toward me.

I received a letter from my friend the day after Christmas. It was dated from the night of my out-of-body experience. He wrote that he had entered his sitting room during his annual holiday party and seen me standing in front of him. He exclaimed in surprise and asked why I was there instead of in Florida. When he tried to shake my hand, I vanished. He was afraid that some misfortune had happened to me and begged me to write at the first opportunity.

I trembled as I read the letter. Here was confirmation that my out-of-body trip had been a true experience and not a fever-induced dream. I showed the letter to my wife and then sat down immediately to answer it and allay the fears of my friend.

I am not so worried about death now, having experienced it once already. I know when my time comes, I will be welcomed into that eternal light by the loving voice who sent me back to finish my work here on earth.

10

A Sprig of Mistletoe

They met under the mistletoe.

He was a young scholar, newly returned from a trip abroad. She was a young debutante in her first season, a blushing beauty whose piquant charm and merry intelligence had made her the toast of Boston. When the scholar saw her, chatting with her friends between dances, he was smitten. Noting the mistletoe hanging above her, he swept into the group and bestowed a kiss upon her cheek with a loud smack that was heard across the entire ballroom. As quickly as he came, he was gone, jesting with friends as they made their way into the dining room. The young debutante stared at his retreating form with wide eyes and parted lips while her friends dissolved into giggles and older matrons glanced knowingly at one another.

A year later, they met once again under the mistletoe: he in evening dress and she in a wedding gown. The mistletoe hung above them in the great hall of the groom's mansion as they exchanged their vows. Holly branches decorated the walls and mantelpiece, and the room was awash with the smells of a delectable Christmas feast. The father of the bride beamed upon the assembled guests, who watched with pleasure as the

A Sprig of Mistletoe

bride and groom promised to love one another until death parted them.

When the ceremony was complete, the guests flowed into the dining room and sat down to a Christmas feast as fine as ever was held. They toasted the bride and groom; they laughed and made merry; they told stories of Christmases past and planned for Christmases yet to come. The blushing bride was the star of it all, with her long white gown and shining eyes. The groom could barely take his eyes from her face long enough to take a bite, and those watching doubted if he knew what food he put into his mouth.

A sprightly tune called the assembly into the ballroom, where the groom waltzed dreamily with his new wife. Then everyone swept onto the dance floor or called for a drink or sank into comfortable chairs to gossip. More than one youth, inspired by the bride and groom, stole a kiss under the mistletoe that evening.

The evening grew late, and the last dance was announced. But the merry bride was not yet ready for her wedding festivities to end. "Let us play a game," she called to her friends, eyeing her groom with a flirtatious smile over her shoulder. "I will hide, and you must trace me to my secret place."

"I will track you to the world's end, my lovely bride," the groom said, stealing yet another kiss under the mistletoe. He pulled a sprig and tucked it behind her ear, a promise of the night to come. She blushed and giggled, then scampered away on eager feet, waving to him once from the doorway before gathering her bridal skirts and vanishing into the hall.

The bride's friends made a great deal of noise, counting down the moments until it was time to search for her. Everyone laughed and called as they went from room to room, searching under tables and behind curtains. Several groomsmen invaded the kitchens and were chased out by the chef. "She is well hidden! But we will find her," the guests told one another.

The groom went patiently into each room in turn, looking in every nook and whispering enticingly into each corner, describing the pleasures to come when he carried her away from her hiding place. The guests scoured the downstairs once, twice, thrice before heading upstairs to the private parts of the house. The bride was nowhere to be found.

Finally, the groom called loudly: "Where are you hiding, my darling? I am lonesome without you, my blushing bride!" There was a moment of silence while everyone listened for her response. But none came.

The parents of the bride were alarmed. This simple game at the tail end of the wedding eve was no longer simple. Where was their playful daughter? She had longed for this day for months. Why would she hide herself now that her dream had come true?

The game took on a frantic edge as groom, parents, and guests searched the mansion from the top floor to the bottom. The servants looked in every room, every hallway, to no avail. The bride could not be found.

The guests scattered to their various chambers or took their leave, speculating all the while at the disappearance of the bride. Had she run away from her groom? Or had some accident befallen her? The parents rushed to their house, hoping their daughter had forgotten some trinket and gone to retrieve it. But the bride was not there.

The groom searched frantically all night, and all the next day. The bride's family too sought high and low, day after long day, week after eternal week. The groom tore apart the house and grounds. He searched the streets, the parks, and far out into the country, fearing that his bride had fallen and knocked her head. "She is wandering in a daze and does not remember who she is," he insisted. "She would never leave me. Of this, I am positive." Fearing for his sanity, his physician finally had to sedate him to get him to take some rest.

Long past the time her family gave her up for lost, the groom still sought for his bride. It wasn't until Christmas Eve a year later, on the very hour when he had exchanged vows with his bride, that the groom ordered his servants to pack up her clothes and take his wife's hope chest—still lying unopened in her small dressing chamber—and store them in the attic. Then he went abroad to grieve.

For many years, the mansion was rented to outsiders while the scholar toured the world, trying to mitigate his grief with intellectual pursuits. When a decade had passed, the scholar felt the call of his childhood town and sent word to his servants that he would be coming home. The family retainers were overwhelmed with joy when they heard of his impending return. The rooms of the mansion were dusted, floors polished, flowers strewn everywhere. The scholar's favorite meal was set to roasting in the kitchens on the day they welcomed him home.

Ensconced in his study after a fine meal, the scholar dozed in front of the fireplace. And dreamed that his lovely young bride was standing before him, dressed in her wedding gown.

"You must trace me to my secret place," she said urgently. "I will hide. I will hide." Catching up her gown in one hand, she disappeared into the hall.

The scholar woke with a start and was on his feet in an instant, racing into the hall as if it were still the eve of his wedding and not a decade later. He caught a glimmer of white on the grand staircase and chased after it. The footmen stared at one another in amazement, and then followed, certain that their employer must be in trouble.

The scholar glimpsed a white hem turning one corner, then the next. He increased his speed, unaware that the upstairs maids had joined the footman in this made-up game of chase. He spotted a white mist climbing to the third floor, then flitting through the servants' quarters and up the attic staircase. By the time the scholar threw himself through the attic door, panting with fatigue, the entire staff had joined the hunt. They piled in behind him, and for a solitary moment, the shimmering figure of the bride appeared clearly before them all. She hovered over her large, dust-covered hope chest. "You must trace me to my secret place," she whispered sadly. Then she vanished.

"Oh, dear God," the scholar groaned, his limbs atremble. He hastened to the chest and fell on his knees before it: frightened of what he would find, knowing he must look.

Behind him, the butler shouldered aside the servants and came to stand at his back. "Let me do it, sir," he begged.

"It is my task," the scholar whispered hoarsely. "This is the one place I did not look."

With shaking hands, he turned the key in the lock and raised the lid. A withered body lay moldering within, still dressed in a wedding gown of white. Scratches marred the inside of the chest where the bride had tried to claw her way out of her prison after the lid slammed shut, trapping her within. Tucked behind her rotting ear was a sprig of mistletoe.

11

The Blue Room

I bumped into my childhood friend Percy Arnold at a Christmas ball when I was at home on leave from the army. Percy was the great-grandson of an immigrant who made his fortune in railroads upon coming to the United States. However, his father had been cast off when he married someone deemed unsuitable by the family, so Percy's parents started a new life in our town.

I was the eldest child of an attorney who lived next door to the Arnolds. Percy was a delicate child with a heart condition, schooled at home for much of his childhood. We became best buddies and did everything together. Percy gained some needed strength and happiness in the years in which I was his main companion. And to everyone's surprise, Percy's father, who had inherited his great-grandsire's knack for business, started his own shipping business and made even more money than the family that cast him off.

Percy was delighted to see me, and I him. I could see immediately that he still suffered from the disease that plagued his childhood. He was too frail, tall and thin with a wan complexion. But his dark eyes sparkled when he saw me, and we retreated to a corner and drank the evening away, talking over

THE BLUE ROOM

old times while the debutantes whirled around on the dance floor and our hostess shot us frustrated glances from time to time. In hindsight, it was probably very rude of us to deny the local debutantes of two eligible bachelors at once. But we didn't think of that until much later.

When Percy learned that my parents were away and I planned to spend Christmas at a hotel, he would not hear of it. "Come spend Christmas with me and my cousin," he cried. "Frank is the new head of the American branch of the Arnold family. He wrote this autumn to apologize for the way the Arnold family treated my parents and asked me for a reconciliation. Frank owns the family mansion out in the country, and from what he's told me, they do a fine Christmas celebration. He told me to bring my friends, so I know he'd be delighted to have you."

I accepted the invitation gladly. A Christmas house party sounded much better than a sparse bachelor dinner at a hotel, no matter how fine the decorations.

"The house should have a particular appeal to you, James," he added. "Since it is haunted. Are you still collecting ghost stories, or has your childhood fascination with that topic waned after joining the army?"

"Quite the reverse," I chuckled. "I'm an old army man now, and I've seen some supernatural things that would curl your hair, my friend. Not that your hair needs any help in that regard!"

Percy frowned in mock fury, and then laughed.

Christmas Eve found me standing in front of an old country house that had seen better days. I was surprised by the condition of the home, and Percy told me in confidence that his uncle, Frank's father, had gambled away all the railroad money and

Frank had been forced to sell off most of their land to maintain the house and grounds in their current form.

Percy's cousin Frank Arnold, older than us by a decade, greeted us at the door with the formal air of a nobleman. He turned us over to his housekeeper, who gave us adjoining rooms in the old tower. My room was finely appointed, but the rugs and curtains were showing their wear, and the room had an air of genteel dilapidation about it, which was disappointing compared to Percy's elegant family home in the city.

The rest of the party arrived later that afternoon, several couples from wealthy neighborhood families and several bachelor friends of Frank. Dinner that night was late and not very appetizing. Frank couldn't afford the quality of service that characterized the lifestyle of my friend. We said nothing, of course. The company was witty, the holiday decorations lovely, and the wine cellar was exceptional, a leftover from a better time.

Adhering to an old Christmas Eve tradition, when we were all settled around the hearth for our postprandial drinks and dessert, Frank told us the ghost story for which the house was famed.

About a decade before the American Revolution, a wealthy younger son of an English nobleman came to America. He purchased land and built this very mansion, which was to be his family's seat in the New World. Then he sent word for his betrothed to come at once, so they could be married and start their new life in this land of opportunity. But she spurned him and eloped with a Scottish laird she met during his absence. Embittered, the young nobleman retreated to his new house, swearing that he would never marry. He spent the next decade amassing wealth and lands, ignoring local society, and cultivating friendships with the local bachelors. He even started a men's club, like White's in England, to keep the local ladies at bay.

His downfall came when a lovely young woman from a local Tory family was thrown from her horse in front of his house. She was injured and carried to his door since it was the closest home. In the days that followed, as the young woman slowly recovered under the care of the local physician, the nobleman fell in love. After a whirlwind courtship, the couple married, and Lady Joan moved into the grand mansion. The nobleman had her bedchamber decorated in blue, which was her favorite color.

It was the early days of the American Revolution, but the wealthy nobleman was mostly shielded against the horrors of the war, which the British were certain to win. The nobleman lived in a bubble of happiness. He had a lovely bride, a beautiful home, friends, wealth, occupation. What more could a gentleman wish for? When England defeated Washington's troops once and for all, his joy would be complete.

Christmas was rapidly approaching, and the nobleman commissioned a new ring for his bride. Lady Joan had beautiful hands that he loved to kiss, and it was his intention to put the ring on her finger at midnight when the church bells tolled on Christmas Day. The beautiful ruby he'd selected was burning a hole in his pocket on Christmas Eve as he rode his horse down the lane toward the mansion. He could not wait to see his bride's eyes light up when she opened the box.

A movement at his wife's window caught his eye, and the nobleman halted his horse. The pane was thrust up, and a man slipped through the opening. He turned and kissed Lady Joan's right hand—the hand for which the nobleman had just purchased the ruby ring—and then shimmied down the tree growing outside the window.

The nobleman sat frozen in disbelief. His hands tightened so hard on the reins that his horse tossed his head uncomfortably. Anger seized the nobleman. All the rage he'd felt when he was jilted the first time overwhelmed him as he realized he'd been cuckolded again. Drawing his sword, he rode in a frenzy toward the intruder, who fled in terror when he heard the nobleman's shout of rage. With a single swipe of his blade, the nobleman cut the man's head from his shoulders. Then he galloped to the front door, leapt from his horse, and thundered upstairs to confront his wife.

They met in the center of the Blue Room, the nobleman screaming in anger at her infidelity, and Lady Joan shouting that he'd just killed an innocent man. The intruder was her Tory brother, who was fleeing from the revolutionaries and had come to say goodbye to his only sister. He had climbed out the window so no one would know he was present and alert Washington's soldiers, Lady Joan claimed. She was not believed.

In her agitation, Lady Joan wrung her lovely hands together, and the nobleman was struck with a terrible idea. Thrusting his wife down onto the floor, he cut off her right hand, which bounced once and rolled under the bed. The nobleman threw the box containing her Christmas gift after it. Then he strode out of the mansion and rode away to one of his many properties, leaving his wife to exsanguinate on the floor. Lady Joan screamed a curse at his retreating figure, saying death would come for him, and for any unworthy person like him who slept in the Blue Room. "They will bear the mark of my severed hand," she choked, "and die within the year."

It was proved after her death that Lady Joan had told the truth. Her husband had killed her Tory brother, and he was brought to trial and hanged for the murders. The mansion was sold, and the new owners quickly found that the Blue Room was cursed. Guests who stayed in the chamber frequently woke to find the ghost of a fair lady figure hovering above them, staring at them with reproachful eyes. Some guests also felt a burning touch upon their shoulder. Those who suffered the touch of the dead hand invariably died within the year. Or so claimed the storytellers.

"Is it true?" asked one of the women breathlessly. She was snuggled tightly against her spouse on the couch, her eyes wide. "Has it happened to one of your guests?"

"It has," Frank said solemnly. "About five years ago, a friend of mine named Sammy Briggs wished to sleep in the Blue Room to see if the ghostly tales were true. That night, he was awakened by a cold presence that hovered beside the bed, staring at him in reproach. A hand pressed against his shoulder, searing him with pain. In the morning, there were three red finger marks burned into his flesh."

"Did he die?" gasped the neighbor woman.

"He was tossed from his horse three months later, and perished," Frank said.

Everyone exclaimed in horror, except Percy, who laughed.

"It's all nonsense and you know it Frank," he said. Frank grinned back at him.

"But it makes an excellent story," he replied, and the whole company relaxed, reassured by their banter.

At this juncture, the housekeeper burst into the room, wringing her hands, and calling for her employer. "Oh, Mr.

Frank, the lantern fell over in Mr. Percy's room and set fire to the bed curtains. The whole room is in a shambles. What shall we do? All the other guest rooms are taken!"

Percy laughed. "Nothing easier, Mrs. Polk. Put me in the Blue Room. No one is in there."

"Oh, but Mr. Percy, the ghost will get you," Mrs. Polk cried.

"Nonsense," Percy said, draining the last of his glass and setting it down on the table. "Let's get me moved over there." He stood and bowed to his host. "Thank you for a lovely evening, Frank. Merry Christmas, all."

I stood too. "I'll help you, old man," I said, and followed my friend out of the room. We followed Mrs. Polk upstairs and transferred Percy's belongings into the Blue Room. Once the housekeeper was gone, I confronted my childhood friend, whose wan face and stiff gait spoke to me of pain and distress that he was keeping in check.

"I'm not letting you stay in a haunted room, old man," I said easily. "Not with your heart. The sight of a spirit would undoubtedly be your undoing. Besides, I've always wanted to see a ghost."

Percy frowned at me for a moment. He hated being reminded of his heart disease. He didn't want to seem weak. But he relaxed when he heard my final words. "I see. This is really about ghost hunting, not my heart condition."

"It's about both," I said. "Now be a good lad and listen to your old friend. Take your sleep draught and go sleep in my chamber. The bed is quite comfortable. I'll keep a lookout for the ghost."

Percy called his old friend a couple of unrepeatable names, but he trusted my judgment. He took the sleeping draught and then climbed into the bed in my chamber to get some much-needed rest.

It was long after midnight when I finally settled myself into the Blue Room, which was a bit dusty and worn, but still serviceable. Percy had not understated my interest in the supernatural. I was a keen collector of ghost stories, and Frank's tale had been a fine one. I'd never seen a ghost, although many of my army buddies claimed that they had. I looked forward to what I might see in the Blue Room on the anniversary of Lady Joan's murder. Of course, I wasn't stupid. If I was going to confront a vengeful ghost, I'd have my revolver with me. A gunshot should scare away even the most intrepid ghost, I thought. I had no intention of being marked by a dead hand. I just wanted to see a phantom. I left the lantern burning and lay down on the bed with my revolver under my pillow for easy access. The mattress was quite comfortable, and I quickly drifted to sleep.

Sometime in the middle of the night, I woke in a cold sweat. Something was amiss. A noise, a scent, a change in the air pressure. I didn't know what awakened me, but my heart was pounding, and my limbs trembled. The banked fire offered little light, and I realized that something had extinguished the lantern. Something? Or someone?

I turned on my side and saw a white figure approaching the side of the bed. In the dim light of the fire, I could make out a long dress and a white countenance. For a moment, I was overcome with dread, for this must be the ghost of Lady Joan, returned to the Blue Room on the very eve of her long-ago death. I heard the rustle of brocade as the figure drew closer. Then a hand seized my shoulder and a burning pain rushed through my body. I screamed and wrenched away in panic, fumbling for my revolver. The phantom withdrew from the bed, gliding toward a tapestry on the far wall. Through waves of agony, I lifted my revolver and fired at the terrible figure. The phantom jerked and cried out, then fell with a thump to the floor.

I leapt to my feet, racing out of the bedchamber, and screaming for help. Back in the Blue Room, the phantom moaned horrifically, raising all the hairs on my body.

Doors on both sides of the hallway burst open, and houseguests and servants in all stages of undress came running to my rescue with lanterns, candles, and firearms. I gabbled out my story and bared my shoulder to show everyone the red marks there. As I was speaking, a terrible groan came from the Blue Room. Everyone screamed and retreated further down the hall.

It was the butler who finally coped with the situation. "We'd best see what we can do about the phantom," he said. "Does anyone have a Bible?" A servant retrieved the holy book from the library, and the whole group reluctantly entered the Blue Room, huddling close together and ready to flee at the earliest sign of menace.

Holding the Bible in front of himself for protection, the butler approached the white figure on the floor, and bent down to shine a candle on its face. It was Frank Arnold, dressed in woman's brocade and a wig. By his side was a hand, made out of iron, that was still glowing red hot from the fire. Behind the tapestry, we found the door to a secret passageway, still opened to admit the master of the house after he played his terrible trick on the sleeper he thought was his frail cousin.

Frank was bleeding heavily from a bullet to the chest. They put pressure on the wound, carried him to his bedchamber, and sent for the doctor, but it was apparent that Frank wasn't going to live. Fortunately for me, the local judge was one of the houseguests, and he obtained a full confession from Frank before he died.

Frank had lost all of the family money, and the bank was threatening to foreclose on him. He was Percy's only living relative, so Frank knew he would inherit Percy's fortune if his cousin died without marrying. Frank needed that money to save his house and lands, so he contrived with the housekeeper to render Percy's room uninhabitable and then snuck into the Blue Room to frighten his heart-weakened cousin to death by pretending to be the ghost of Lady Joan.

It was a despicable plan, and it would have worked if I hadn't traded places with my childhood friend. Frank died on Christmas Day, shortly after sunrise. The judge acquitted me of manslaughter, due to the extraneous circumstances surrounding the shooting. The housekeeper who had plotted with her employer to murder his cousin fled the county, never to be seen again.

When Percy woke from his sleeping draught at noon on Christmas Day, he learned that he was the new lord of the manor.

The story was spread through the neighborhood by the scandalized houseguests, and no one knew whether to congratulate Percy or avoid him. He solved the problem by selling the house and returning to his home in the city.

Percy always credited me with saving his life that night. He wasn't wrong. I had the shoulder scars to prove it. But I felt embarrassed whenever he told the tale, so I shrugged off the praise. After all, anyone would do the same if their childhood chum was in danger.

12

Find the Child

The sanctuary was in chaos, which was par for the course during a Christmas pageant rehearsal. The Angel Gabriel was chasing two of the shepherds up the center aisle, one of the Magi was sobbing because someone had taken her fake gold bar, and several sheep were playing a game of Simon Says with Joseph.

I gave a shrill whistle, alerting all the helpers that it was time to line up the troops for rehearsal. Volunteers swept down upon the massed children and brought them to the various entrances, ready for the narrator to begin the age-old tale of Mary, Joseph, and the Christ Child.

Which reminded me. Where was Baby Jesus? The manger was set up in front of the altar, with two chairs and several hay bales beside it. But there was no baby doll in view, and Mary wasn't cradling anything in her costume-clad arms.

Dang it, we'd misplaced the Christ Child. This was probably some kind of cosmic crime, but I didn't have time to go into spiritual philosophy at the moment. I grabbed my phone and made a memo to myself: Find the Christ Child. Then I gestured to the narrator to begin reading the Christmas story, and the Angel Gabriel swept in from the side hallway to speak to the

FIND THE CHILD

Virgin Mary, who was having trouble with her sash and forgot her lines.

Things went smoothly during the first section of the rehearsal. Mary and Joseph traveled down the center aisle, Mary perched atop a wooden donkey on wheels and Joseph rolling them onward toward Bethlehem. The friendly beasts met the holy couple in the stable and sang "Away in a Manger," with a minimum of swatting and sneezing as they jockeyed for position on the hay bales. The Angel Gabriel put in a second appearance with a piano fanfare, and the shepherds flung themselves dramatically under the pews to convey their shock and dismay. Since the script called for their angelic-induced dismay to occur in the left aisle and not under the pews, we were forced to redo the shepherd scene. With pastoral order thus restored, a group of tiny angels surrounded Gabriel and sang "Glory to God in the Highest" while the shepherds ran pell-mell to Bethlehem to see the baby.

"Cue the Magi," I called, since our solo Wise Woman refused to be referred to as a man. "All right folks, head to Bethlehem."

Two Wise People headed up the center aisle, but the third Magi swerved to the right. "Lorenzo, where are you going?" I asked.

"We are supposed to stop by Befana's house and ask her for directions," Lorenzo replied. "But she turns us away, so then we have to find the Christ Child on our own."

The story of Befana was an Italian tradition that dated back for centuries. According to the tale, Befana was a poor old woman who lived in a small, but very tidy house around the time that the Christ Child was born in Bethlehem. As the Magi followed the star toward Bethlehem, a series of storms began dropping rain over the land. After several cloudy nights with no star to guide them, they lost their way. When they saw Befana sweeping her doorstep, they stopped to ask her for directions. Befana told the Wise Men the direction in which the new star could be seen from her doorstep, and, in return, they excitedly shared with her the reason they were following it. When they departed, the Magi asked the old woman if she wanted to join them in their search for the newborn king. But it was cold and rainy, and Befana had too many chores to do at home. So, she declined their offer.

Later that night, Befana was awakened by a bright light. A heavenly voice asked why she had not joined the Magi on their quest. Conscious-stricken, Befana rose at once and baked a pan of her very best sweets as a gift for the Christ Child, then went in search of the Magi. But the caravan had traveled far in the night, and she could not overtake them. Over hill and valley Befana searched for the Magi, but in vain. They were gone. She asked the same question of every person she met: "I must find the Christ Child. Do you know where he is?" But no one could tell her the way. They said: "He is not here, Befana. You must go farther on." So Befana went farther and farther from her home, searching for the Christ Child, but she never found him.

According to the legend, Befana continues her search to this day, an eternal wanderer still trying to deliver her gift to the Christ Child. "I must find the Christ Child," she says to all who meet her. She travels from house to house, seeking the babe in the manger. And she leaves small gifts for good children on Epiphany, in case the Christ Child is among them.

I thought fast and told Lorenzo: "The Magi visited Befana out in the hallway, just before your entrance. So, you can go up the center aisle with the others."

"Okay," he said happily, trotting to his proper place and hauling a big bottle of myrrh to the front, where he dropped it accidentally on Joseph's foot. The pageant continued without further incident, unless you counted the change in the wording of the descant that was improvised by the older boys during the final number. It sounded suspiciously like the lyrics to the number one song currently on the charts. When I frowned, they squirmed and laughed into their songbooks.

It was with relief that I dismissed the whole rascally bunch back to the loving arms of their parents and guardians. If we survived the pageant tomorrow, it would be a miracle akin to the holy birth. Which reminded me, I must find the Christ Child, or the manger would be bare in the morning. Not a good look at Christmas.

I trotted into the church office and called to the secretary: "Bess, I must find the Christ Child. He's gone missing."

"You lost Baby Jesus?" she asked, looking up from her computer.

"Not me, last year's pageant director," I replied. "But I'm tasked with his recovery."

She laughed. "You make it sound like he's been kidnapped."

I made a face: "With the lot out there, it's a possibility we can't overlook!"

My statement reduced her to giggles. Still snorting into her sleeve, she handed me keys to the various closets and the basement. "Good luck with your search!"

I was going to need it. Our church was huge.

I rummaged in the hall closets first, but they were well kept, and no Christmas apparatus appeared within. Well, I knew it couldn't be that easy. With a sigh, I made my way toward the new annex. It was a monstrous construction. I could spend hours looking into every classroom and closet. And don't even get me started on the piles of junk I might have to sort through in the basement.

As I turned the corner into the hallway, I saw an elderly woman in a dark shawl sweeping the floor. She was intent upon her task, a vision of industry. I didn't recognize her from the roster of church volunteers. Then again, our church was so large, it was impossible to know everyone. If she was part of the cleaning crew, she might know where I could find the Christ Child.

"Excuse me," I called to her.

She looked up from her sweeping with a smile that crinkled the fragile skin around her dark eyes. "I must find the Christ Child. He's gone missing from the manger. Do you know where he is? I need to locate him before tomorrow's pageant."

The old lady hummed and set aside her broom. "I am also looking for the Christ Child," she said. "Perhaps we can look together?"

I sighed with relief. "That would be a big help. This church is huge. There are a lot of rooms to go through."

I unlocked the storerooms in the gym, but we only found the tables and chairs we set up for meetings and celebrations. Then we tried the closets in each Sunday School classroom. Still nothing. Well, not nothing. There were crayons and construction paper and those safety scissors that can't cut anything, and half-finished art projects and seasonal decorations for displays and all the necessary detritus for a successful kids' program. But no Christ Child.

We had no more luck with the closet under the staircase, which held Christmas decorations and other holiday paraphernalia.

"He isn't here," I told my stalwart companion, who'd helped me dig through every carton and bag in every closet without complaint. "At this rate, it will take us decades to locate him."

"Centuries," murmured the bright-eyed old lady with her wrinkled cheeks and charming smile. "I'm something of an expert, by now. We must go further."

"Onward," I agreed, pulling out the key to the basement.

We descended into the dim, clammy space under the original building. While the annex was bright, large, and modern, this part of the church was more than a century old. Rummaging around down here was like looking through an antiques shop. I glanced about, feeling a bit daunted by the task, but my companion tapped my arm and gestured to several large boxes tucked into a corner. Some red and green garland was peeking out through an opening that was meant for a handle.

We split the boxes between us. I was neck deep inside a box full of dolls in Christmas costumes from around the world when the woman beside me said: "It is not the real Christ Child, but I'd say it is a fair likeness." I looked her way and saw her holding the doll we used to represent the Baby Jesus.

"You found the Christ Child," I cried, stretching out my hands in delight. She deposited the baby doll into them.

"Not yet. But we did accomplish your task. If only mine was so easy," she replied with a sigh.

I blinked and looked sharply at her. Really looked at her. She was elderly and wrinkled. Her long dark dress and shawl could have belonged to almost any age. And she was soft and fragile around the edges, as if she did not quite share the same dimension as the rest of us.

Befana smiled at me. "Now I must go. I must find the Christ Child," she said, and vanished.

I clutched the doll representing the Christ Child to my heart in shock and stared at the empty place beside me. Or was it empty? A small white plate filled with *pefanino* slowly materialized upon the seat of the chair. The Italian Epiphany biscuits looked just like the ones made by Lorenzo's mother last year for coffee hour on January 5, to represent the gift Befana made for the Christ Child.

What had just happened here? Had the spirit of Befana felt kinship with my search for the pageant Christ Child doll? Is that why she came to help me? It was probably as good an explanation as I was going to get. With shaky hands, I reached out and picked up a *pefanino*. It was still warm, as if it had just been taken from the oven.

I carried the plate of the Epiphany biscuits to the office and shared them with Bess. Then I laid the Christ Child in the manger and straightened up the stable scene, making sure all the props were in place for tomorrow's pageant.

I headed for the sanctuary door, pausing just long enough to turn out the lights. My search was over, but Befana was still looking for the Christ Child. Would she ever find him? Others had located him: in a manger, on a cross, in an empty tomb, ascending into heaven. Why was Befana trapped in this single moment? Was there, perhaps, a deeper meaning to her search? Something I was missing?

I sighed and turned off the light over the manger. I'd be soul-searching for weeks after my supernatural encounter. And maybe that was exactly why it happened.

"Thank you for helping me find the Christ Child, Befana," I called into the dim twilight of the sanctuary. And then I went home.

PART TWO

Powers of Darkness and Light

13

Der Belznickel

My sisters and my baby brother danced about the house, whispering to each other excitedly about the coming of der Belznickel on that snowy December 5 evening, the day before the Feast of Saint Nicholas. According to the stories, the good Saint Nicholas chains up the devil on the eve of his birthday—December 6—and makes him visit all of the children in the village to see if they have been behaving themselves and deserved the attention of *Christkindl.* Those who are good will receive gifts, but those who are naughty . . . well, those children who do not know their prayers or their school recitations or who have been troublesome at home might find themselves whipped with der Belznickel's switch or tied up with his chains, and they will receive coal in their stockings instead of presents.

Of course, I did not participate in the excited whispering or silly romping of the youngsters. I was above such foolishness, having turned twelve on my last birthday. Instead, I peeled potatoes in the kitchen to help our mother with dinner. I heard several pairs of feet stampeding up the stairs and shaking the floorboards over my head, and I sighed a little at all the

DER BELZNICKEL

dramatics. Just then, someone tugged on my skirt, and I looked down at Hans, my three-year-old brother.

"Gretel, will der Belznickel come tonight?" he asked me, his huge blue eyes wide with anxiety. I scooped him up into my arms and gave him a reassuring hug.

"Yes, Hans, he will come tonight," I told him.

And he would too. I had seen Uncle Oskar stashing a dark costume—consisting of raggedy fur-trimmed black clothes, a headband with goat-horns glued to the top, a long whippy switch, and a thick, rattling chain—in the empty stall in the barn about an hour before sunset.

Right after dinner, Uncle Oskar would duck out to "see to the horses," and a few moments later, der Belznickel would make his visit to see if we children had been good enough to receive the attentions of Saint Nicholas tomorrow.

"Will he have a switch and chains? Will he tie us up?" Hans asked.

"Der Belznickel only ties up naughty little boys and girls. But you have been good, so you need not worry," I said. Hans still looked a bit uncertain.

"Were you ever tied up, Gretel?" he asked, fingering my long blonde braid nervously.

"Never. I am always *ein gutes Mädchen*—a good girl," I said a bit smugly. "Der Belznickel will ask us to recite our lessons from school and then will give us some sugar candy."

"Inga said he chased her up and down the hallway last year, rattling his chain," Hans said.

"That's because he found out Inga cheated on her spelling test at school," I said. "She almost got coal in her stocking instead of presents, except she said she was sorry to Mama and

Vater, and that made der Belznickel leave her alone. But you've been very good this year, and so has Inga. There won't be any chasing; just recitations and candy."

This reassured Hans. I put him down and he scampered off upstairs to talk to Inga and my other sisters while I finished the potatoes.

There were fourteen of us at dinner that night—Mama, Vater, my four sisters and three brothers, Uncle Oskar, Aunt Helga, their two children, and me. As the oldest child, I watched over the others and made sure that the babies got fed. Then Uncle Oskar slipped out to "feed the horses," and the grownups exchanged happy grins over the little children's heads.

The first sign that "der Belznickel" was approaching was a loud, rude banging on the front windows. Hans and Inga screamed when a soot-covered face with long black whiskers was pressed against the glass. Then the front door burst open and der Belznickel rumbled into the parlor, rattling his chains. The children cowered and whimpered and screamed half in fear and half in delight at the raggedy creature with his goat's horns and bag full of something—was it candy or coal? The answer depended on what happened next!

Der Belznickel made all of us—even me—line up in a row in our parlor. Starting with me, we began to answer whatever questions he asked us. He rattled his switch at me and made me quote the scripture passage from last Sunday's church service. Martin—the next oldest—recited a poem he had memorized for school. And so on down the line. Every time we got an answer right, der Belznickel would stomp about in rage because he hadn't tricked us, and the little ones would squeal.

I was distracted from Uncle Oskar's antics by a strange flickering in the lantern light. Something was wrong with Uncle Oskar's shadow. I began watching it as he made Ludwig recite next. When Uncle Oskar lunged one way, the shadow went the opposite way. As I watched, it lifted the chains over its head. The shadow's hands seemed impossibly long, and the fingers looked more like claws. I shivered, chills running over my skin. The horns on the shadow's head were very sharp, and the legs too long. Then the shadow broke away from Uncle Oskar completely, just as Ludwig finished his recitation. As the grownups and children all cheered for Ludwig's success, the shadow slid over the wall like oil and coiled up near the ceiling. Then it opened its glowing yellow eyes and looked straight at me.

I gasped, my heart pounding and my legs shaking. My terror was masked by the happy shrieks of the youngest children, who were watching Uncle Oskar—the pretend Belznickel—stomping up and down the hallway rattling his chains and howling in "anger."

I faced the opposite direction, toward the corner of the room, watching the real Belznickel slide down the wall, his shadowy form slowly solidifying into a short, twisted figure dressed in coal-black fur with a broken nose and vibrant yellow eyes. No one else noticed him as he slithered like a snake past my parents and Aunt Helga and began stalking the hallway at Uncle Oskar's heels.

My stomach was twisted into a knot. I wanted to run away and be sick, but I couldn't tear my eyes off the evil figure that stopped before my cousins and watched as they spelled several difficult words at Uncle Oskar's request. Johanna stumbled a bit, and der Belznickel gave an audible chuckle and seemed to grow larger within the shadow of my Uncle Oskar. When Johanna recovered herself enough to finish spelling her word successfully, der Belznickel shrunk in size and frowned. Occasionally, the creature would dart a look at me and give me a twisted grin.

Little Hans was the last one in line, and he was terrified. He stared up at large Uncle Oskar and couldn't breathe a word.

"Have you been a good boy?" Uncle Oskar asked, taking pity on the small figure. Hans nodded fervently, and Uncle Oskar patted his head and handed him a boiled sweet. Behind him, der Belznickel stomped in rage and then dematerialized, becoming a thick black oozing mass that gradually sank back into Uncle Oskar's shadow and disappeared.

I staggered a little, as if a weight had been released from me, and stared suspiciously at the shadow, wondering if the creature was really gone for good. My siblings and cousins were mobbing Uncle Oskar, demanding sweets from "der Belznickel" since they had all done so well with their recitations.

As he handed out the treats, I heard a knock at the window. I looked out into a pair of glowing yellow eyes in a twisted face.

"I will see you again next year, Gretel," der Belznickel hissed through the glass. "Try not to be too good."

I screamed then and fainted, toppling to the floor before Vater could catch me. They told me later that all was confusion in the parlor for several minutes, during which time Uncle Oskar slipped away. I awoke to the stinging sensation of smelling salts and clung to Mama and cried as if I were no older than Hans. My siblings and cousins laughed at me, their own fear forgotten, but Mama hushed them, realizing that my terror had nothing to do with Uncle Oskar. She sent them away to the kitchen to eat their sweets. When they were gone, I told Mama and Vater and Aunt Helga what I had seen and heard.

Vater nodded his head several times as I spoke, and then said: "*Mein Kind*, I once saw the real der Belznickel too when I was about your age. I will tell you now what *mein Vater* told me then. Der Belznickel is bound by the goodness of Saint Nicholas. If you are a good child—if you do your best and try to be kind and say your prayers—no harm will come to you."

I shuddered, remembering the look on der Belznickel's face when he called my name.

"I will, Vater. I will," I promised fervently.

"I have heard that people who see der Belznickel also have the good fortune to see Saint Nicholas," Aunt Helga added unexpectedly. "*Meine Muter* told me that she saw them both at the Feast the year she turned twelve. Watch carefully tomorrow, Gretel, and you may also see the blessed saint."

The grownups hustled me to bed after that, and Mama tucked me up tight. I was quickly joined by my sisters, who drifted off immediately, but I couldn't sleep. I kept seeing the leering face of der Belznickel before me and hearing him call my name. Downstairs, the grandfather clock chimed the hours away as the house grew quiet and the adults went to bed.

As time ticked its way toward midnight, a moonbeam shone through the window, shining across the room and dazzling my eyes. Beautiful, it was, and comforting. I slipped out of bed and went to look out at the moon that was turning our room into a shadowy and mysterious place. It was as bright as noon outside, and the trees and bushes cast serene shadows over the snowy landscape. Then I saw, riding up to the road on a dashing white horse, a bearded man dressed in red with white fur lining his hood. It was Saint Nicholas. Running before him and muttering darkly was der Belznickel. The grim little figure seemed more comic than scary now, bound by his rattling chains and forced to dance to the whim of the good saint behind him.

For a moment, the saint paused in front of my house and looked up at my window. He raised a solemn hand to me, and I smiled and waved back. Then he spurred his horse away down the road, der Belznickel scampering ahead of him like a little black dog, and they disappeared into the dazzling snowscape under the light of the full moon.

With a soft sigh, I returned to the comfort of my bed, sensing that this was the last time I would see either der Belznickel or Saint Nicholas. And I knew something else too. I knew that I had nothing to fear from the grim little creature, not now, not ever. I fell asleep with a smile on my face and woke the next morning to the joyful shouts of my siblings on Saint Nicholas Day.

14

The Christmas Dance

DES MOINES, IOWA

Marie Elise was furious with her beau for being late, tonight of all nights. It was the night of the big holiday dance, and Ned had promised that he would pick her up in his sleigh an hour before the party started so she could dance every dance. He'd promised! Here it was, nearly eight o'clock, and the dance started at eight thirty. And still no sign of him!

She glared at the clock, then went back to the mirror to straighten her hair.

"If you'd stop pacing your hair would stay in place," her mother called from the fireside chair. She was knitting placidly, ignoring her daughter's anger.

Marie Elise glared at her mother and started pacing back and forth, back and forth across the sitting room, her long skirts swirling against the carpet as she stalked to and fro. "I will never forgive Ned for making us late to the dance," she exclaimed. "Never, never, never!"

"You are acting like a two-year-old child," her mother remarked, turning the heel on the sock she was knitting. "Has it occurred to you that Ned might not be coming tonight?"

THE CHRISTMAS DANCE

Her daughter stopped in her tracks, her pretty red mouth dropping open in shock. "Not coming! Of course he's coming! I'm the loveliest girl in school and he's the handsomest boy. He'd never go to the dance with someone else!"

Her mother eyed her wryly. She and her husband had made a mistake in spoiling Marie Elise. They had indulged her too much as a child and were now repenting for it. She was vain as a kitten and her head was empty of everything but frills and frocks and boys. She expected everyone and everything to fall in with her plans and threw a tantrum any time something didn't go her way.

"I meant that it is extremely cold tonight, and snow is falling," her mother said. "Ned might not be able to make it through the storm."

"Of course, he can. What's a little cold and snow, compared to the wonders of the dance!" Marie Elise whirled around the room, demonstrating a fancy waltz turn as she spoke. "Anyway, I don't care if Ned comes or not," she added with a pout of her red lips. "I would go to the dance with anyone who will take me. I'd even go with the devil himself if he asked me politely. Just so long as I go to the dance!"

"Marie Elise! Watch your tongue!" Her mother was shocked. She'd raised her daughter to be a God-fearing, churchgoing young woman. Such talk of the devil was sacrilegious. And maybe even dangerous, a tiny voice murmured at the back of her mind.

"I wouldn't mind if the devil did take me to the dance," Marie Elise said boldly. "It would make me stand out from the other girls!"

Before her mother could remonstrate further, they heard sleigh bells approaching. Marie Elise exclaimed excitedly and ran to look out the window into the snowy lane. A fancy sleigh was approaching, pulled by two midnight-black horses that looked like ink blots against the white snow.

"Oh! Ned has rented a fancy sleigh for the night," Marie Elise cried happily. "I told you he wouldn't take anyone else to the dance. He knows I'm the loveliest girl in the whole county! Maybe in the whole state!" She danced around the room for a moment, long skirts swirling about her. Then she ran to get her cloak and muff as footsteps sounded on the porch and the knocker rapped against the front door.

"Get the door, mother," Marie Elise called as she scrambled into her outdoor clothing.

Her mother sighed, put down her knitting, and went to the door. She opened it with a smile, for she rather liked Ned, who was always polite to her and her hardworking husband. The open door revealed a very handsome stranger standing there with hat in his hand, snowflakes melting on his dark curly hair.

"Good evening," the mother said politely. "May I help you?"

Before the stranger could speak, she was shoved rudely aside by Marie Elise, who exclaimed: "I won't forgive you for being so late, Ned Bl . . ."

Marie Elise stopped mid-sentence when she saw the stranger, who reached past her to steady her poor mother, who'd fallen against the doorframe.

"Who are you?" Marie Elise cried rudely. Then she blinked, realizing this dark stranger was twice as handsome as Ned. She primped her long gold curls and added in her sweetest tone: "Can I help you with something? Are you lost?"

"I am here on behalf of Ned," the dark-haired, dark-eyed charmer said smoothly. "He was called away to see a dying relative and asked me to take you to the dance tonight in his place. He didn't want to disappoint you."

"How very kind of him," gurgled Marie Elise, "And even kinder of you." She cooed the last three words and stepped out on the porch to take his arm. In the doorway, her mother frowned.

"What is your name, sir? Who are your folks?" she asked. "Won't you come in and get acquainted with us? Marie Elise, we should invite him in to warm up."

The mother stared keenly at the stranger, feeling uneasy. His hand, when he steadied her, had been too warm. His touch had burnt her, even through the thick layers of her scarlet winter dress. And there was a red glint in his eye that she did not like. Her daughter had just invoked the name of the devil, and now here was this stranger standing on their doorstep with his reddish eyes and haughty smile.

"Mother! Don't fuss," Marie Elise exclaimed, flushing with anger, her pretty red lips pursed sourly.

"*You* have nothing to fear, Madam," the stranger said with an odd smile. Was she the only one who heard the emphasis on the first word, the mother wondered?

"Marie Elise. Remember what you have just said," the mother said, reaching desperately for her daughter. Marie Elise stepped away from her parent, glaring with real hatred in her blue eyes.

"I said it once and I'll say it again. I am going to the dance no matter what! I'd even go with the devil himself if he asked me politely. Just so long as I go to the dance!"

"And will you accompany me tonight, my fair lady?" asked the stranger with a charming smile and a bow.

"Sir, I will," Marie Elise replied with an equally charming smile. She curtseyed, turned her back upon her mother, and walked with her escort down the steps and out to the waiting sleigh. The mother stared fearfully after her, and then buried her face in her hands as her daughter stepped up into the seat and the man drove away to the tintinnabulation of sleigh bells.

Marie Elise exclaimed excitedly over the fancy sleigh, the fine night-black horses, the falling snow: so pretty, so delicate. The handsome stranger laughed and spoke sweetly to the girl of fancy balls attended, far-off places visited, exotic sights seen. The trees flashed by in the light of the carriage lanterns, blurring slightly with their speed. Marie Elise had never had a merrier sleigh-ride. Her escort was so charming, so handsome, so debonair. Ned was nothing compared to him.

Marie Elise hugged her cloak around her as the air grew colder and still colder. She snuggled her hands deeper into the fleece and edged a bit nearer to her escort for warmth. For the handsome man *was* warm. The only warm thing on this cold, cold night.

The sleigh twisted and turned down the long, windy road, and Marie Elise's breath turned to frost with every exhalation. Yet the heat emanating from her escort made the seat uncomfortable to sit on, and the side of Marie Elise that was closest to the stranger was extremely hot, as if she were sitting next to a roaring fire. She edged away from him until she was pressed against the freezing-cold side of the sleigh. Now one side of her was freezing and the other side of her was too hot.

"Sir," she exclaimed suddenly, realizing belatedly that they had traveled a long distance without arriving at their destination. "I believe we must be lost! The dance cannot be this far out in the country."

"Lost?" the man said in a deep voice that echoed with the crackle and spit of flames. "No, we are not lost Marie Elissssssse." He hissed the final syllable of her name like a snake, and the bare skin of her face heated painfully and tightened across her bones as if she'd spent too much time in the sun. "In fact, we have just arrived!"

The scenery around them blurred, and suddenly they were pulling up in front of the large hall, decorated to the rafters with Christmas candles, mistletoe, holly, and evergreens. The stranger helped her down and sent a servant to park the sleigh and stable his horses.

As soon as Marie Elise walked into the room, the music stopped, and everyone turned to look at her. It was like a fairy tale come true. As one, all the men surged toward her as if she were the embodiment of beauty and desire, then froze mid-step when her handsome escort appeared at her side. Marie Elise's dashing new beau held out his hand. "Dance with me," he said.

She hesitated, remembering the uncomfortable heat that had emanated from him during their cold ride. But what Cinderella denied her prince the first dance? Thrusting aside her unease, Marie Elise graciously accepted. The man led her out on the dance floor. The music sprang up at once, and the crowd whirled joyously around the hall. Marie Elise found herself dancing better than she ever had before. Slowly the other couples stopped dancing to watch them. Marie Elise was elated. They were the center of attention.

Then the man spun Marie Elise around and around. She gasped for breath, trying to pull her hand away from his hand, which burned her skin. She tried to step out of the spin, but her partner spun her faster and faster, until her feet felt hot, and the floor seemed to melt under her. Marie Elise's eyes fixed in horror on the man's face as he twirled her even faster. She saw his eyes burning with red fire, as he gave her a smile of pure evil. For the first time, she noticed two horns protruding from his forehead. Marie Elise gasped desperately for breath, terrified because she now knew with whom she was dancing.

The man in black spun Marie Elise so fast that a cloud of dust flew up around them both, hiding them from the crowd. Her hair and clothes caught fire from the unbearable heat pulsing from the man beside her. The devil laughed as she screamed in agony. Then Marie Elise, body in flames, fell suddenly down and down into a looming black pit that ended, far below, in brimstone.

When the dust settled, Marie Elise was gone. The man in black bowed once to the assembled townsfolks, then vanished. The devil had come to the Christmas dance, and he had spun Marie Elise all the way to hell.

15

Chicken Thief

SAN DIEGO, CALIFORNIA

Don Pedro sat bolt upright in bed. Dona Luisa turned over. "What is it, husband?" she asked.

"That no-good fox is after our chickens again," Don Pedro exclaimed. "Just listen to them squawking! There will be none left for our Día de Los Reyes Magos celebration!"

He jumped out of bed and ran to get his rifle. Stalking outside in his nightclothes, Don Pedro hurried toward the chicken coop. In the shadowy darkness, he could see a dark figure creeping away with a struggling chicken. Taking aim, he shot once, twice, three times. The figure fell to the ground and the chicken escaped, squawking in terror and running in circles.

Dona Luisa appeared with a lantern in her hand. "Did you get the fox?" she asked.

"Shot him three times," Don Pedro said proudly. "Right there."

He walked over to the dark form on the ground and turned it over with his foot. Then he gasped in fear. It was a man, not a fox! He recognized the chicken thief as Felix Maria, a shifty outlaw who had never done an honest day's work in his life.

"My husband, you have killed him!"

CHICKEN THIEF

"He was stealing my chickens!" Don Pedro protested.

Dona Luisa wrung her hands. "*Madre de Dios*! They are going to hang you for this! We must do something!"

"What can we do?" asked Don Pedro.

Dona Luisa brightened. "My husband, I have an idea!" she exclaimed.

Enrique sat bolt upright in bed. His wife, Dona Estella, turned over sleepily. "What is it, husband?" she asked.

"There is someone trying to break into this house!" Enrique exclaimed.

"A *bandido*!" Dona Estella cried. Enrique jumped out of bed and ran to get his rifle. Creeping around the outside of the house in his nightclothes, he saw a dark figure leaning menacingly against his front door. Taking aim, he shot once, twice, three times. The figure fell to the ground.

"Enrique, are you all right?" cried Dona Estella from inside the house.

"I have shot the *bandido*!" Enrique shouted. "Bring me a light!"

Dona Estella appeared with a lantern in her hand. Enrique walked to the dark form on the ground and turned it over with his foot. Then he gasped in fear. This was no *bandido*! It was Felix Maria, a shifty outlaw who had never done an honest day's work in his life.

"My husband, you have killed him!" cried Dona Estella.

"He came menacing my house at night!" Enrique protested.

Dona Estella wrung her hands. "*Madre de Dios*! They are going to hang you for this! We must do something!"

"What can we do?" asked Enrique.

Dona Estella brightened. "I have an idea!" she exclaimed.

Tom sat bolt upright in bed. Something he had eaten for dinner had not agreed with his stomach, and nature was calling. The cowboy jumped out of bed, dressed, and hurried to the privy behind the bunkhouse.

It was occupied by a stranger.

"Hurry up, I ain't got all day!" Tom said to the stranger, rocking back and forth from foot to foot in his predicament. The stranger did not respond.

"Some of us have got to go, partner!" Tom insisted.

The stranger did not answer. Tom drew his pistol.

"Get off the pot, Jack, or I'll shoot you!" the cowboy shouted, now in dire straits.

The stranger did not respond. Tom grabbed the stranger by the hair, knocked his head against the wall, threw him down on the ground outside the privy, and shot him in the leg for good measure. Then he jumped over the doorstep and pulled the door closed.

When he got out of the privy, the cowboy walked to the dark form on the ground and turned it over with his foot. Then he gasped in fear. He recognized Felix Maria, a shifty outlaw who had never done an honest day's work in his life.

"Gosh almighty, I've killed the feller," Tom exclaimed. "They are going to hang me for this! I gotta do something!"

Then the cowboy had an idea.

Jorge had had a long night. His bar was full of drunken cowboys and greedy gamblers, all of them getting an early start on the Three Kings' Day festivities. It was a typical holiday scene. But

Jorge felt a bit uneasy about Felix Maria, the shifty outlaw who had never done an honest day's work in his life. The man was sitting at the bar with a ghastly grin on his face. He could barely keep himself upright. Jorge was sure he must be drunker than a lord. The strange thing was, Jorge could not remember serving any drinks to the outlaw that night.

Just then, a belligerent gunfighter turned to Felix and said: "I don't like the way yer looking at me, mister. You just stop staring at me and go back to yer drinking, if you know what's good fer you."

Felix grinned vacantly at the gunslinger and didn't respond.

"I'm warning you, mister. Keep staring at me and you'll regret it!"

Felix didn't respond.

The gunslinger whipped out his pistol and let fly—one, two, three times. Felix kept grinning as he slowly fell off the bar stool and hit the floor.

Jorge peered down at the outlaw. "You just shot an unarmed man," he told the gunslinger. "They are going to hang you for this!"

The gunslinger shifted uneasily. "I just nicked him!" he said. "The sawbones will patch him up in a jiffy. What happened, see, is he fainted on account of he was so afraid of me. I'll just take him over to the doctor's place, lickety-split."

The gunslinger picked Felix up and carted him outside. Then he spotted the decorated wagon that would hold the Nativity scene in the Día de Los Reyes Magos parade, an annual town event that took place on the evening before the holiday. It gave him an idea.

Juan was feeling uncomfortable with the Nativity scene on his Día de Los Reyes Magos parade float. It was lovely and authentic, with Mary and Joseph seated around the manger and the angel praying on top of the stable the village carpenter had constructed for them. The sheep and donkey nodded their heads, baaing and braying. The littlest shepherd squealed excitedly and waved to his friends as the float moved slowly down the parade route. It was the shifty outlaw Felix Maria, who had dressed as one of the shepherds, that was causing Juan's unease. Felix Maria leaned against the wall of the fake stable with a ghastly grin on his face as he gazed down into the manger. Juan was convinced that Felix Maria was drunk and using the props to keep himself upright. For the life of him, Juan could *not* remember the outlaw volunteering to be one of the actors on his float. But there he was. Juan hoped that the stable wall concealed Felix Maria from the cheering crowd. He made a very spooky shepherd.

Juan was relieved when he reached the end of the parade route. The cheerful Nativity actors jumped down from the wagon, laughing and joking with one another. Juan thanked them and then climbed back onto the wagon seat, glad to be done for the year. Then he saw Felix Maria, still propped against the stable wall, staring vacantly at the doll in the manger.

"I suppose I should take you home," Juan grumbled. "Drunken fool!"

He turned the wagon down the road leading to Felix Maria's small house and asked the horses to trot. Suddenly, the wagon lurched as the wheel hit a pothole. Felix Maria went flying over the side of the wagon. The horses panicked at this unexpected complication. They reared and lunged forward. To

Jorge's horror, the back wheels of the parade float rolled right over Felix Maria!

Gasping in panic, Juan jumped down from the wagon and hurried to the dark figure lying on the road. He turned Felix Maria over with his foot. Then he gasped in fear. It looked like the man was dead.

"Mister, I saw the whole thing," the gunslinger said, riding up on his horse. "You ran him over with your wagon. They are going to hang you for this! You are supposed to watch out for drunks!"

"What am I going to do?" Juan asked the gunslinger.

"I don't know, mister. That's your problem," the gunslinger replied, and rode off into the darkness.

Juan picked up the corpse of Felix Maria and put it in the back of the wagon. He drove away from town, wondering what to do. Then he had an idea.

It was the night before Día de Los Reyes Magos, and the children were fast asleep, exhausted by all the fun they had at the parade. Dona Luisa spent the hours before bed icing the King's Cakes and answering the letters the children had written to the Los Reyes Magos, while Don Pedro crept into the bedrooms to replace the hay the children had placed under their beds for the camels with gifts for the morrow.

It was quite late when Dona Luisa and Don Pedro finished with their preparations for the next day's holiday feast and family gathering. Tired but happy, they retired to their room and snuggled down into their warm bed.

They had just blown out the lantern when a terrible squawking arose from the back yard. Don Pedro sat bolt upright in bed. Dona Luisa turned over. "What is it, husband?" she asked.

"That no-good fox is disturbing our chickens again," Don Pedro exclaimed.

He jumped out of bed and ran to get his rifle. Outside in his nightclothes, Don Pedro hurried toward the chicken coop. In the darkness, he stumbled and almost fell over the figure of Felix Maria, the shifty outlaw who had never done an honest day's work in his life.

Dona Luisa appeared with a lantern in her hand. "What is it, husband?" she asked.

"Felix Maria is back," said Don Pedro.

Dona Luisa wrung her hands. "*Madre de Dios!* We must do something!"

"What can we do?" asked Don Pedro.

Dona Luisa said: "Husband, I think you will have to pay another visit to our friend Enrique!"

16

Baker's Dozen

So, my grandson, you want to hear a story about the old days, eh? Would you like to hear the tale of how your grandfather met Sinterklaas (Saint Nicholas), who is the patron saint of merchants, sailors, and children? Very well then, I will tell you!

Back in the old days, I had a successful bakeshop in Albany. My only rivals were the *knikkerbakkers*—they were the bakers of marbles—and they could not hold a candle to me. I had a good business, a plump wife—your grandmother—and a big family. I, Volckert Jan Pietersen Van Amsterdam, was a happy man.

But for all my good fortune, I was a little spooked by the stories I had heard of witches and their evil craft. 'Twas my greatest fear in those days, the fear of being bewitched. I was a good, law-abiding man who went to church each Sunday with my family, but I could not shake my fear of witches. I think now that this was caused by my lack of trust in Saint Nicholas to look after me and my family properly. And perhaps I was unconsciously aware that my stingy nature in my dealings with my fellow man might someday cause me a problem.

Trouble did come to my door the last day in December of 1654. I had spent the whole month making New Year's cakes,

BAKER'S DOZEN

gingerbread, mince pies, and *speculaas*—molded spice cookies of Saint Nicholas. It was these cookies that started my troubles the day before the New Year began.

It had been a very busy day in my shop. I was relaxing behind the counter and having a second glass of spirits to celebrate my gains when a sharp rap came at the door and an ugly old woman whom I had never seen before entered my shop.

"I wish to have a dozen New Year's cookies," cried she, pointing to my Saint Nicholas cookies that were sitting out on a tray.

"My good Vrouw, you do not need to shout so loudly. I am not deaf," I chided her as I counted out twelve cookies.

The old Vrouw's eyes narrowed when she saw the cookies. "Only twelve?" she asked.

I knew at once what she wanted. I was an educated man. I had heard about the bakers in England who gave thirteen loaves to their customers rather than a round dozen. Back in the thirteenth century, the English had imposed strict regulations upon their bakers regarding the weight of a loaf of bread. However, my grandson, it was impossible to ensure that every loaf of bread would meet the regulation weight, as any good baker could have told you. In those days, it became the custom for English bakers to add an extra loaf to their dozen to guarantee that they made the weight for their order. This was a long time ago, but some English bakers still abided by this custom.

I did not know how this ugly, uneducated old woman had heard about the English baker's dozen, but somehow, she knew the custom and wanted me, a Dutchman, to abide by it. I was appalled! Without paying for extra, she wanted more?

"I asked for a dozen cookies, and you only give me twelve," the woman said.

"A dozen *is* twelve, my good Vrouw, and that is what I have given you. That is what you ordered and that is what you pay for."

"I want another. I ordered a dozen cookies, not twelve," said the old woman.

I tell you, my grandson, I was upset. I was an honest man. I always gave my customers exactly what they paid for. But I was also a thrifty man. To give away something for nothing? This was against my nature.

"Do I look like an Englishman?" I shouted. "I have a family to support. If I give away all my cookies, how can I feed my family? A dozen is twelve, Vrouw, not thirteen! If you want another cookie, you can go to the devil to get it!"

My grandson, this was a foolish thing for me to do. I, who was so afraid of being bewitched, had just shouted at an ugly old woman of whom I knew nothing.

"Very well," said she, and left the shop without taking the cookies.

Was I afraid? Not then. I was a fool, and so I raged to myself as I closed the bakeshop and stomped home to tell my wife about the crazy old Vrouw who wanted something for nothing.

That was the beginning of my bad luck. The next day, my cakes were stolen out of my shop, and the thieves were never found. Then my bread refused to rise. For a week, every loaf of bread I made was so heavy that it fell right through the oven and into the fire. The next week, the bread rose so high that it actually floated up the chimney. I was frightened when I saw the loaves floating away across the rooftops. That was the first moment I believed myself bewitched. I remembered the old woman then and wondered if she was a witch.

I was upset that a witch would put a spell on me just because of a single cookie. The next week, when the old Vrouw appeared in my shop, demanding a baker's dozen of the latest batch of my cookies, I cursed her soundly and sent her back to the devil from which she came. The old witch left my shop, and I slammed the door behind her.

Things became worse for me. My bread soured, and my *olykoeks* (donuts) were a disgrace. Every cake I made collapsed as soon as it came out of the oven, and my gingerbread children and my cookies lost their flavor. Word was getting around that my bakeshop was no good, and one by one, my customers were falling away. I was angry now, and stubborn. I was a God-fearing, churchgoing man, and no witch was going to defeat me. When she came to my bakeshop a third, and then a fourth time to demand a baker's dozen of Saint Nicholas cookies, I told her to go to the devil, and the last time I locked the door behind her.

After that day, my bakeshop was haunted by invisible spirits. While I was baking, invisible hands would take bricks from the oven and throw them at me until I turned black and blue. Each time my wife visited the shop, she was struck with deafness that would last for hours. Rents and tears would appear in my children's clothing, and no matter how often my wife toiled to mend them, they would reappear within moments.

My customers began to avoid my cursed shop, even those who had come to me every day for years. Everything I baked was either burnt or soggy, too light or too heavy. Finally, my family and I were the only ones eating my baking, and my money was running out. I was desperate. I took myself to church and began to pray to Saint Nicholas, the patron saint of merchants, to lift the witch's curse from myself and my family.

"Come and advise me, Saint Nicholas, for my family is in dire straits and I need good counsel against this evil witch who stands against us," I prayed. Then I trudged wearily back to my empty shop, wondering what to do.

I stirred up a batch of Saint Nicholas cookies and put them into the oven to bake, wondering how this lot would turn out. Too much cinnamon? Too little? Burnt? Underdone? To my surprise, they came out perfectly. I frosted them carefully and put my first successful baking in weeks onto a tray where they could be seen through the window. When I looked up, Sinterklaas was standing in front of me.

I knew him at once, this patron saint of merchants, sailors, and children. He was not carrying his gold staff or wearing the red bishop's robes and mitered hat that appeared on the figure I had just frosted on my cookies. But the white beard and the kindly eyes were the same. I was trembling so much my legs would not hold me, so I sat down on a stool and looked up at the saint standing so near I could have touched him. His eyes regarded me with such sadness it made me want to weep.

"Volckert Jan Pietersen," Saint Nicholas said softly, "I spent my whole life giving money to those in need, helping the sick and suffering, and caring for little children, just as our Lord taught us. God, in his mercy, has been generous to us, and we should be generous to those around us."

I could not bear to look into his eyes, so I buried my face in my hands.

"Is an extra cookie such a terrible price to pay for the generosity God has shown to us?" he asked gently, touching my head with his hand.

Then he was gone. A moment later, I heard the shop door open, and footsteps approached the counter. I knew before I looked up that the ugly old woman had returned to ask me for a dozen Saint Nicholas cookies. I got up slowly, counted out thirteen cookies, and gave them to the old woman, free of charge.

She nodded her head briskly. "The spell is broken," she said. "From this time onward, a dozen is thirteen."

She pointed to the tray of Saint Nicholas cookies and said, "I ask you, Volckert Jan Pietersen Van Amsterdam, to swear by the saint that you will be more liberal in the future."

I swore readily, remembering the saint's words to me moments before. And from that day to this, my grandson, I have given generously of my baking, and of my money, and thirteen will always be, for me, a baker's dozen.

17

New Year's Hunting Trip

MACKINAW CITY, MICHIGAN

The first sign of trouble came when Father tried to hire a native guide to take us deep into the northern woods for our annual New Year's hunting trip. It was just the three of us—Father, Jonathan, and me, Richard, the younger son. Our family lived in the big city, where Father worked as an attorney, so we didn't need to hunt. We had plenty of money to purchase whatever provender we needed. But the New Year's Hunt was a family tradition several generations strong. Attendance—according to Father—was mandatory. So, every year, he hired a guide to take us deep into the wilderness for a week to hunt and trap.

But this year was special. We were taking several weeks off to venture into the wilds of the American Frontier. It was by way of being a celebratory trip, since Jonathan had been taken into Father's very successful law practice as a junior member, and I had just been accepted into university. I was just a gangling youth in those days, all long arms, long legs, awkward wrists, and floppy hair, who didn't look too promising. Nobody would have guessed, seeing me then, that I would top six-foot-six in my bare feet and have the brawny build of a lumberjack by the time I finished growing.

NEW YEAR'S HUNTING TRIP

Mother waved us off from our fancy city home with tears in her eyes, fearful of what might happen to us in the terrible dark woods of the north. She'd heard stories all her life of fierce wolves and hungry bears, as well as dark spirits that would possess a man. Father laughed away her fears. We would have a whole slew of local guides to accompany us on our icy trek, and we would return triumphant, with more deer meat than the family could eat in a year. But Mother wasn't so sure. She had a bad feeling about the trip, and she was frightened she would lose a member of her family to the evil denizens of the north.

The first part of our trip was relatively easy—the weather was cold but unseasonably dry. So little snow had fallen that our stagecoach made good time as it traveled northward to the settlement. Folks there assured us that we would have no trouble hiring a few tribesmen to guide us on our trip. And it was true that each man that Father approached listened to him eagerly for the first few minutes. Then his face would freeze partway through Father's speech, his mind pulling away from the conversation even though physically he did not move. And each conversation ended with a sharp negative shake of the head and with each potential guide walking away.

"What are you saying to them, Father?" asked Jonathan in that half-jovial, half-superior tone that I hated. Don't get me wrong, I do love my brother. But he was already as cynical a creature as ever walked the Earth, and vain to boot—though frankly, with his too-short frame, popped-out fish eyes, and slicked-back curly dark hair that perpetually shed white flakes of dandruff onto his shoulders, he really had no excuse for vanity.

"I don't understand it," Father said slowly. "Every time I tell the guides that we want to hunt deer up near the great lake, they break off negotiations. They tell me that the hunting is no good there and walk away."

"The winter hunting *is* no good near the lake this year," a deep voice rumbled from behind us. A massive tribesman stepped out of the shadowy corner of the inn where we had repaired to eat our dinner and figure out what to do. "You should hunt somewhere else this season."

But Father turned stubborn. First Mother and now this! He wanted to hunt up by the lake. Two of his partners had gone hunting by the lake last season and had raved about it ever since. This was Father's first chance to go, and he was going to take it, even if it meant finding our way north without a guide.

The tribesman listened to his ranting in grave silence, dark eyes hooded against us. Now and then he asked a question or uttered a short sentence, and I was impressed by his clarity of thought, deftness of speech, and superior intelligence. If this man ever studied law, Father and Jonathan wouldn't stand a chance against him in court.

The man's eyes were suddenly upon me, and we studied each other intently for a moment as Father raged, egged on by Jonathan. Some sort of silent message passed between me and the tribesman, an acknowledgement of Father's stubbornness and Jonathan's vanity and the foolish pride of both that was sending us into danger. The fact was that nothing either of us said would change their minds. That moment of understanding sealed a lifelong friendship between me and the tribesman, who told us to call him Hawk.

The upshot of our conversation was that Hawk hired on to guide us north to hunt and trap along the shores of the great lake. He brought along two other men to carry our winter hunting equipment and keep camp for us: one was a French-Canadian trapper called Jean-Claude, and the other a wiry little Irish chap who gave his name as O'Toole. Nothing else. Just O'Toole. Together, the six of us headed north. Jonathan tried to get Hawk to tell us why the other tribesmen were reluctant to make a potentially lucrative hunting and trapping journey to the north, but Hawk wasn't talking.

We reached the shores of the lake after a week of travel, canoeing the rivers where the fast pace of the water kept them from icing over and portaging across the land the rest of the way. It was a strange winter. The land around us was devoid of heavy snow. Any random snow squalls we encountered were short-lived and left little precipitation behind. With such an easy winter, we should have seen many hunters venturing into this fertile hunting ground. Yet we had encountered no one along the way. No lumber scouts. No settlers. No tribesmen. It was as if everyone had fled the vicinity. The thought made me go cold. *Fled from what?* I wondered.

Hawk set up camp in a small clearing on the icy lakeshore, and soon we were gathered around the fire, eating beans, and planning our first big hunt. Father and Jonathan talked excitedly about some bear tracks they had seen not far from our campsite and discussed various tracking methods with Jean-Claude. O'Toole—the expedition cook—hummed an Irish jig under his breath as he made another pot of coffee. The hunting talk didn't interest him. His duty was merely to stay in camp, do some ice fishing, and prepare food and coffee at a moment's notice when we returned from a hard day's hunt.

On the far side of the fire, Hawk sat like a stone, dark eyes unfathomable. I watched the huge tribesman, who appeared to be sniffing the air, like a rabbit trying to scent the presence of a predator. The thought made me shiver. I accepted a mug of coffee from O'Toole and took a seat beside our guide.

"My mother says that dark spirits haunt the North Woods," I said softly, under cover of the lively conversation between my father and Jean-Claude.

"Your mother is a wise woman," said Hawk, his tone equally low.

"Is something here with us?" I asked, my voice calm. In front of me, I watched the mug of coffee in my hands begin to tremble.

"I do not know," Hawk said reluctantly. "There have been rumors that something has come down from the far north. The elders of many tribes have seen it approaching in their dreams."

He broke off, staring into the fire.

"I myself have seen it," he said at last, his voice barely audible. "In a vision last summer."

I started, the hot coffee spilling out over my hand. I ignored the stinging sensation and whispered: "What have you seen?"

Hawk closed his eyes briefly, and his face grew grim.

"Wendigo," he whispered and then rose abruptly and walked off into the darkness.

Seeing his retreat, Jonathan smirked from the other side of the fire and said: "Don't scare off our local guide, little brother, unless you learned how to track bear at your boarding school."

"Knock it off, Jonathan," I said, rising and wiping my wet hand on my breeches. "I'm going to bed."

I crawled into the tent and settled down among the heavy blankets and balsam boughs laid ready for the night, my mind churning. *Wendigo*, Hawk had said. What was a Wendigo?

I'd never heard the term before, but the tone in which it was uttered had filled me with a nameless dread, and I was uncomfortably aware of being very far from civilization up here in the bleak splendor of the remote North Woods. I felt small and insignificant amid the beautiful, merciless forest with its massive trees, snowy drifts, and huge wild beasts. I stayed awake for a long time, trembling under the covers. It was only the familiar sound of my father's bass voice singing some of the old French-Canadian *voyageur* songs with Jean-Claude that finally calmed my fears and lulled me to sleep.

I was awakened during the night by a sound in the tent. I froze, my heart pounding against my ribcage, and held my breath, trying to identify the sound. Then Father let out a second loud snore, and I let out my breath in a sigh of relief. I nudged him a little, and he turned over and settled down again, breathing softly. I lay on my back, staring uneasily up at the dark roof of the tent, unable to get back to sleep. The night was unusually quiet. There was no sound save the soft whisper of the breeze. Within the primeval winter forest surrounding us was the silence of death.

Slowly, I became aware of a sickly, almost sweet smell, like that of rotten fruit. I stiffened, remembering the way that Hawk had been sniffing the air. I drew the scent into my nose, body tense with fear, but already the smell was fading . . . fading . . . gone.

We woke early, ready to track bear in the dim light of dawn. We found the fire burnt down to coals, the food still tied up high in a tree, and O'Toole gone. Vanished into thin air. At first, Father thought the Irishman was playing a joke on us. All his gear was still in the tent he shared with Jean-Claude, so he couldn't have gone far. We called and searched the surrounding forest. It was Hawk's keen eyes that spotted the snowy footprints leading toward the area we'd designated for our privy—and not back again. He looked at the hard-packed snow, at the icy rocks, at the dirt, his mouth grim. The shadow of a known horror passed over his face. "We must leave here at once," he said suddenly, straightening to his massive height and staring down at my father. "O'Toole was taken."

I remembered the strange silence in the night and the sickeningly sweet odor I had smelled. I envisioned the cook stepping out of his tent into that wintery silence to answer the call of nature. And being taken by . . . what? That was the question Father was asking. What had taken the cook? A bear? A cougar?

"Wendigo," said Hawk grimly and began packing up our gear.

When he heard the word *Wendigo*, Jean-Claude gasped and crossed himself. Glancing toward him, I saw that the tough old *voyageur* was shaken to the core. He peered this way and that into the snowy woods, his brown eyes searching for something that obviously terrified him, breath coming in short, sharp gasps, face as pale as ice.

Then he too leapt forward and rapidly began dismantling the tent.

"Stop, man, stop!" roared Father. "Why must we leave? What is this Wendigo? I paid good money for this trip. And I'm not leaving until we find O'Toole!"

I shivered with nerves. The French Canadian's terror was catching. Suddenly, I passionately wanted out of this place. Jean-Claude turned a face of livid terror toward Father. "You won't find O'Toole," he said fiercely. "Not if the Wendigo got him. You can stay here if you want. I'm leaving."

"We're all leaving," said Hawk, looming up behind Jonathan and making him start with fright. "Right now."

And we left, our gear mashed into packs and canoes any which way. Father and Jonathan were trembling with rage and irritation, but they followed the tall tribesman and the French Canadian because they had no choice. We could never find our way alone in this vast, untamed wilderness.

We portaged with the canoes more than two miles before striking a place in the river that was free of ice. Just before we pushed off, Hawk spotted something in the brush. He stalked forward, disappeared into the trees, and returned with the torn body of O'Toole. The cook's head lolled on a broken neck, his ribs had been split apart, and his guts torn out. There were teeth marks covering his throat and one side of his broken body. It was obvious that he had been eaten by something big.

My father's protests died away at the sight of O'Toole. He hustled Jonathan and me into a canoe with Jean-Claude and pushed us off so quickly that I barely caught a glimpse of the poor dead cook before we were navigating the rough current in the center of the river. It was only when we were rapidly traveling downstream, me and Jonathan and Jean-Claude in one boat and Hawk and Father and O'Toole's blanket-wrapped corpse following us in the other, that I ventured to ask Jean-Claude about the creature that had killed the cook.

"Yes, what *is* a Wendigo?" Jonathan added loudly. Too loudly. Jean-Claude glanced about wildly and hushed him. Jonathan repeated his question sotto voce. This time, the French Canadian answered him.

"Cannibal," he whispered as we paddled at top speed down the river. "Dark spirit of the woods with a craving for human flesh. The more the Wendigo eats, the more it craves. It is tall and gray green like a rotting corpse, all cracked skin and clotted blood and pus. You smell them first—the sickly-sweet odor of decay—and if they catch you, they eat you, like poor O'Toole." I gasped aloud when he described the smell, and he gave me a sympathetic smile, misunderstanding my fear. I had smelled the Wendigo last night. It had passed right beside my tent!

"Sometimes," Jean-Claude continued over the splash of the river, "a Wendigo will call a man by name. When it calls, you must obey. The Wendigo will run with you across the treetops, across the sky at blinding speed until you bleed beneath the eyes and your feet burn away to stumps. Then it drops you to the ground like a bird dropping a fish on a rock. Any man that runs with a Wendigo, becomes a Wendigo himself."

Regrettably, Jonathan—the hard-headed attorney—laughed when he heard this. "That's just nonsense," he said derisively. "It's obvious that O'Toole was eaten by a bear. Wendigo. Ha! Just a rural myth."

Jean-Claude clammed up after that and spoke not a word to either of us until we beached the canoes at dusk. Hawk wanted to keep going through the night, but Father insisted that we stop and rest. We had traveled many miles downriver during the day, and surely had left the beast that killed O'Toole far behind. This would have been true enough if we were dealing with a living creature. But I wasn't as convinced as Jonathan was that we were. Wendigo—dark spirit of the north country—the creature that my mother feared would kill her family. Was it only a myth? If not, then we were dealing with a creature that could fly through the air. To such a creature, what were a few miles?

I could see Hawk and Jean-Claude felt as I did. They left most of our belongings in the canoes, ready to launch out onto the river immediately if something happened. Jean-Claude set up two of the three tents while Hawk made a large fire and cooked a simple meal for us. Father and Jonathan—the two practical attorneys—sat on one side of the fire, talking in low tones about the superstitious nonsense that had ruined our special New Year's hunting trip. I sat with Hawk and Jean-Claude on the other side. We ate in silence, listening to the cold wind blow through the pines as night settled over the forest around us. We were still five days from the nearest settlement, I thought, a tremor of fear shaking my body. Five days.

As soon as he finished eating, Jean-Claude fled into the tent to sleep, fear pulsing from his whipcord hard body. I am not sure what shelter a tent would provide from a determined Wendigo, but it seemed to offer comfort to the French-Canadian trapper. When he was gone, I said to Hawk: "Tell me about your vision. Did you see the Wendigo kill O'Toole?"

Hawk shook his dark head. "No, Richard," he said. "I saw myself . . ." he hesitated, staring into the fire.

"You saw yourself . . ." I prompted when the silence grew too long.

"I saw myself killing a Wendigo to save someone's life," he replied at length, avoiding my gaze. My eyes nearly popped out of my head.

"They can be killed?" I gasped. "How? I thought they were dark spirits?"

"A Wendigo has a heart made of ice and snow," said Hawk. "If you pierce that heart with an arrow of fire, the Wendigo is no more."

My eyes went to the bow and quiver of arrows that were always strapped to Hawk's side. I had wondered why he favored them over a gun. Now I knew.

We followed Jean-Claude's example and settled into the tents for the night. No one would be tempted to leave the shelter tonight for any reason. Not after what happened to O'Toole. Father placed himself in the center of the tent, between me and Jonathan, to protect us, I think. Anything coming through the door would get him first.

We lay awake a long time, pretending to sleep. I imagined Jean-Claude and Hawk lying awake in the next tent, listening . . . listening. Finally, Jonathan started to snore, and Father after him. The familiar sound relaxed me, and I was nearly asleep when my nose was assailed by a sickeningly sweet scent. I sat bolt upright in terror. Wendigo! I wanted to shout for Hawk. But in that moment, a violent movement shook the tent. Father woke with a startled shout, and Jonathan rolled over, trembling with shock. From somewhere outside came a thunderous voice. It came from overhead rather than beside us. The volume of sound was immense and wild, full of an abominable power that was as sickly sweet as the smell of the demon. It called a man's name.

"Jon-a-thannnnnn."

And Jonathan was on his feet, leaping past Father, bumping into the tent pole, then plunging through the canvas door into the frigid winter night. He was running so fast his body seemed to blur in the dim firelight. As he ran, he was joined by an immensely tall gray-green figure. They disappeared into the trees before Father or I could draw a breath.

I think I screamed. I know Father did. We bumped into each other twice before we managed to scramble from the tent. "Jonathan," Father bellowed. "Johnny! Come back, son! Come back!"

He ran toward the woods in the direction taken by his elder son, but Hawk caught him and pulled him back.

"There's nothing you can do," the tribesman said. "The Wendigo has taken him."

"Let me go! I must find my son," screamed Father. It took all the massive tribesman's strength to hold him back.

"What can you do in the dark, *mon ami?*" asked Jean-Claude, who was frantically throwing wood on the fire to strengthen the blaze. His face was as white as a ghost. "At least wait until morning to look for him."

"Jonathan panicked when the wind struck our tent," Father said defiantly. "That's all. There is no such thing as a Wendigo." He stared from one face to the other, and the grave compassion he saw there broke his defiance. "He will come back to camp. You'll see," he continued almost pleadingly. "I'm staying right here until he returns. I will not leave here without my son!"

"We did not ask you to leave," said Hawk, laying a massive hand on Father's shoulder.

And then, from somewhere high above us, we heard a terrible cry. "Oh! Oh! My feet of fire! My burning feet of fire!" It was Jonathan's voice. Father gasped and dropped to his knees, as somewhere above the trees, Jonathan shrieked: "Oh! Oh! This height and fiery speed!"

A terrible rush of wind whipped the treetops, as if a storm were approaching. Then all was silence, and the stench of decay slowly faded from the riverbank. Father, his face gray with pain, looked up into Hawk's dark eyes. "I will not leave without my son," he repeated. The tribesman nodded his understanding, his eyes brimming with sorrow.

We sat by the fire, silently waiting through the long hours of a winter night for the icy dawn to come. None of us spoke. What could we say? We had all heard that horrified wail. But there was nothing we could do to help Jonathan during the long darkness of night.

I dozed a couple of times, leaning against my grief-stricken father for comfort. Toward dawn, I was awakened by the sound of a rushing wind. Something dropped heavily through the trees beside the river. In the dim gray light, I felt Father stiffen beside me and saw Hawk leap to his feet, bow in one hand and arrow in the other. The tip of the arrow was wrapped in cloth, and he pushed it into the fire as I sat up, rubbing my eyes.

Then I saw him. Jonathan came lurching toward us through the half-light, his step faltering, uncertain. At least, I think it was Jonathan, though it seemed a ghastly caricature of the brother I had known all my life. The face was twisted, features drawn about into strange and terrible proportions, skin loose and hanging, as though Jonathan had been subjected to extraordinary air pressures and tensions. The skin below his eyes was red with blood, and his feet were blackened stumps. My nose caught the penetrating odor of rotten fruit as my brother lurched toward the clearing, his eyes fixed on Father.

There was something about the look in his eyes . . .

I didn't think; I just reacted, shoving myself in front of Father as Jonathan suddenly sprang forward with supernatural speed, his mouth a gaping black hole as he screamed in hunger and fury. There were claws at the ends of his hands, curved and vicious, and his eyes burned as he slashed out at me, intent on the kill. Then a fiery arrow winged its way over my shoulder from Hawk's bow. It caught Jonathan in the chest, penetrating his icy heart, stopping him a mere two feet from my body. He fell to the ground, momentum sliding him forward until he reached my feet. He screamed in agony, and gray-green smoke billowed out of his mouth and rose to the treetops.

Behind me, Hawk sent another flaming arrow up toward the swirling gray-green mist that was forming into a tall man-shaped figure that looked like a rotting corpse, all cracked skin and clotted blood and pus. The Wendigo rose with a terrific rushing noise that whipped the trees with hurricane force. But the flaming arrow rose faster, smashing right through the center of the Wendigo. It screamed and exploded into flames. At my feet, Jonathan's body also burst into flames. Jean-Claude and Father pulled me backward, away from the danger, as my brother and the Wendigo burned to death before my eyes.

Father wanted to bury Jonathan in the family plot back in the city, so we wrapped what was left of him in a deerskin and laid him in the canoe beside O'Toole. We traveled as quickly as we could back to the settlement, while around us, the snow-clad forest slowly stirred back to life after the defeat of the Wendigo.

Jean-Claude left us as soon as we reached safety, glad to be rid of us and the terrible memory of that aborted New Year's hunting trip. But Hawk accompanied us to the stagecoach and

18

A Gift of Saint Nicholas

MANHATTAN, NEW YORK

Claas Schlaschenschlinger was a wealthy cobbler living on New Street in New Amsterdam. He was a contented bachelor who could afford eight—eight, mind you!—pairs of breeches, and he had a little side business selling geese. He cut quite a figure in New Amsterdam society, and was happy being single, until he met the fair Anitje at a dance! She was as pretty as a picture, and Claas fell head over heels for her. He was not her only suitor, by any means. The local burgomaster was also courting the fair Anitje. But the burgomaster was a stingy, hard man, who frowned upon pretty dresses and poetry, dancing, and merrymaking. Life with such a husband seemed grim to the lovely, whimsical Anitje. In the end, Anitje gave her heart and hand to Claas.

At first, Claas and Anitje were very happy and prosperous, raising many geese and roly-poly children. But the burgomaster was a vengeful sort of fellow, who began a series of "improvements" to the local neighborhood, each costing more than the last. He charged heavy fines for families that did not comply with his demands. The burgomaster twisted regulations so that the Schlaschenschlinger family was required to make

A Gift of Saint Nicholas

every single costly improvement on his very long list. And so, he whittled away at their wealth until their money was all but gone.

Then the burgomaster invited a blacksmith to move into their area. The fellow began repairing shoes and boots with hobnails, so that the townsfolk's footwear lasted a year or more. The money the cobbler had earned from making small repairs dried up overnight, which left Claas, Anitje, and their six children as poor as church mice.

"We will have to move away," Claas told his wife sadly. "There must be another place where a man of my talents can earn a good living."

"Husband, you are right," Anitje replied, wiping away her tears with her apron. "But let us stay here one last Christmas, so the children have a happy memory to take away with them. It is only another day or two."

Claas agreed to this plan. God willing, their money would stretch through Christmas Day.

But he reckoned without the burgomaster, who dropped by the cobbler shop to demand yet another unneeded but expensive improvement that must be made at once to the property where Claas lived with his family. The work was tedious and unnecessary, but Claas bit his tongue and did it anyway, for the fine he must pay if the work remained undone was heavier than the cost to make the improvement. It left him with no cash whatsoever to buy Christmas presents for his family. What little money he had barely paid for food.

By Christmas Eve, all the Schlaschenschlinger family could afford for their holiday feast was a meal of cold bread and cheese. There was no roast goose, no presents for the morrow, and no hope of remaining in their home after the holiday. They would have to sell house and land to have enough money to begin again somewhere else. But, as Anitje said bracingly, they had one another, and that was wealth indeed.

As afternoon faded into dusk, Claas sat in his favorite chair and looked at the faces of his family, wondering if there was anything he could sell so that he could provide them with a nice meal for Christmas Day. Then he remembered a fine pipe that he found in one of his stockings on a long-ago Christmas morning in Holland. It was a fine pipe, too good for a mere cobbler. Claas knew even then that such a gift could only be from Saint Nicholas himself.

Claas leapt up and went to dig through an old chest until he found the pipe. As he unearthed it from under a pile of clothes, a draft of cold air came from the open front door. Claas scolded his children for playing with the door and went to close it, but found the doorway filled by the merry, round figure of a stranger.

"Thank you, thank you, I will come in out of the cold," said the man, stomping in the door and taking a seat by the poor excuse for a fire that blazed in the hearth.

The family gathered around the white bearded old fellow as he tried to warm himself. He scolded them roundly for not keeping the fire hot. Claas's cheeks heated with shame. Reluctantly, he admitted that they had nothing left to burn. The little old man patted his arm sympathetically. Then he broke his fine rosewood cane in two and threw it on the fire. The cane blazed up merrily, heating the whole room, and singeing the hair of the cat, which leapt away with a yowl of indignation, making everyone laugh. It was hard to be sober around this merry old man, who made sly jokes, told riddles, and sang songs.

After sitting for half an hour with the family, the old man began rubbing his stomach and gazing wistfully at the cupboard.

"Might there be a bite to eat for an old man on this Christmas Eve?" he asked Anitje. She blushed with embarrassment for such a lack of hospitality. Her voice was barely a whisper as she admitted there was nothing left in their cupboard. "Nothing?" said he, "Then what about that fine goose right there?"

Anitje gasped, for suddenly the smell of a tenderly roasted goose filled the room. She ran to the cupboard, and there was a huge bird on a platter! She also found pies and cakes and bread and many other good things to eat and drink. The little boys and girls shouted in delight, and the whole family feasted merrily, with the little white bearded old man seated at the head of the table.

As they ate, Claas showed the old man the pipe he meant to sell. "Why that pipe is a lucky pipe," said the old man, examining it closely. "Smoked by John Calvin himself, if I am not mistaken. You should keep this pipe all your days and hand it down to your children."

Finally, the church bells tolled midnight, and the little old man cried: "Midnight! I must be off!"

Claas and Anitje begged him to stay and spend Christmas with them, but he just smiled merrily at them and strode over to the chimney. "A Merry Christmas to you all, and a Happy New Year!" he cried. And then he disappeared.

Ever afterwards, Anitje and her daughters claimed they saw him go straight up the chimney, while Claas and the boys thought he kicked up the ashes and disappeared out the door.

The next morning, when Anitje was sweeping the fireplace, she found a huge bag full of silver, bearing the words "A Gift

19

Eavesdropper

This is, he told himself as he carefully set the long ladder against the side of the barn, *probably one of the stupidest things I have ever done.* The ladder thumped against the wall below the hayloft window with a soft thud, and the legs of the ladder slipped a bit on the snowy ground. He steadied the ladder and then blew on his bare hands to warm them.

The snow had come as a surprise that Christmas Eve morning, falling just long enough to coat the ground. He blamed the snow for the argument he'd had with his wife that afternoon. Miranda had started singing songs about white Christmases and had chattered about Christmas traditions and folktales. He hadn't minded her sudden zealous talk about the holiday until she mentioned her favorite legend.

"And they say," Miranda had said as she tied a ribbon around a gift for his mother, "that at midnight on Christmas Eve, the cattle kneel in the barn and speak to one another."

He had gaped at her incredulously and then had started laughing as he turned back to hang another ornament on the Christmas tree. Miranda had flushed and snapped: "It's true!

147

EAVESDROPPER

My mama told me she heard them herself one Christmas Eve when she went to the barn to check on a sick heifer."

In retrospect, he probably shouldn't have called her mother a lunatic. That was a mistake Miranda would not soon forgive. They had argued for nearly an hour, forgetting the present wrapping and tree trimming. Then they had each gone away to sulk and were still rather cold with each other when they gathered again for dinner.

Miranda had taken herself to bed early with a headache. He had gone to bed an hour later and had lain beside his wife fuming about the silly argument. Finally, he had crept out of bed, careful not to wake her, had dressed in warm clothes, and come out to the barn. He wasn't sure what his motive was. Did he want to prove that Miranda was wrong, or that he was? He just knew he wouldn't be able to sleep until he'd seen for himself whether or not the cattle spoke at midnight on Christmas Eve.

Outside, he pulled the ladder out of the shed and carried it to the barn so that he could sneak up on his cows. According to the tale Miranda had spun, the cows did not appreciate eavesdroppers on their holiday conversation. When—as a young girl—Miranda's mother had arrived unexpectedly at the barn at midnight and heard the cows speaking to one another, she'd slipped into an empty stall to listen. But an unexpected sneeze had betrayed her presence, and the animals had stopped talking immediately when they heard her. Nary a word was spoken the whole time she was examining the sick heifer, and talk did not resume until she had exited the barn. Though Miranda's mother had stood for several minutes with her ear pressed to the door, she could not make out what the animals said.

He crept up the ladder as silently as he could, feeling foolish as all get-out for hiding from his own cows, and slipped through the open window. The hayloft was fragrant with the smell of dusty hay and sweaty cow. Thankfully, it was warmer in the loft than outside. He blew on his hands again and then lay down on the rough gray boards next to a fairly large knothole directly over the cow stalls and covered himself with hay to keep warm.

After waiting for what seemed like more than an hour, he grew drowsy and irritated, wanting his cozy bed and an unbroken night's sleep. It had to be after midnight, he thought, glancing at his wrist. To his chagrin, he realized that he'd left his watch in the house. He frowned and sat up. And then froze.

Below him, the cows started to low, one after another. He lay back down and pressed his eye to the knothole. One by one, the cows knelt in their stalls, and he saw his horse do the same. And within their soft calling he could make out real words. At first, he could not understand more than a word or two here and there. Then he heard the cow underneath his hiding place say to its neighbor: "I am afraid our poor master will not live out the year."

"Oh, dear," exclaimed the neighboring cow. "What a pity."

He covered his mouth to prevent himself from gasping aloud. What were they saying? That he was going to die? He was in perfect health! His pulse started pounding, and he broke out in a cold sweat. No! He must be dreaming. He'd fallen asleep under the warm hay and dreamed the cows below him were speaking to each other.

"What will poor Miranda do without him?" he heard another cow ask as he jumped to his feet and hurried over to the window. He didn't care if this was a dream or not, he wanted to get away from the barn as fast as he could. He slipped through the window, his feet fumbling for the first rung of the ladder. And then his sweating fingers slipped on the sill, and he felt his body falling toward the ground. He twisted desperately, trying to grab onto the ladder. Then he smashed head-first into the icy ground. A brilliant flash of light went right through his head, and he felt his neck snap. The world went dark.

Miranda went looking for her missing husband the next morning and found him dead beside the barn. The ladder to the hayloft window told her the rest of the story.

After word got around about the tragedy, people in those parts never again tried to eavesdrop on the talking cattle at midnight on Christmas Eve.

20

The Bachelor

Advent Season was a big deal in our small town. Each year, the prominent families tried to outdo one another in holiday dances, socials, Christmas caroling, and overall festival cheer. It was my favorite season. And this year, in addition to the usual festivities, we had a brand-new bachelor to introduce to our local society.

According to the land agent, a man named Gelu Vlach bought the vacant general store for a princely sum and planned to open it in early December. Rumor credited Mr. Vlach with additional virtues including a handsome face, a well-muscled figure, and a bachelor status, which set the gossips abuzz with excitement.

The land agent's wife invited Mr. Vlach to her annual Christmas tea celebration as soon as they were introduced. Not coincidentally, this event was cohosted by her eldest daughter, who had just reached a marriageable age and was currently seeking a life partner. She was not the only hostess interested in Mr. Vlach. Every matchmaking mama in town sat up and took notice when they learned that a rich new bachelor would shortly be arriving on the local social scene.

The Bachelor

I first observed the new bachelor through our parlor window on the evening he moved into the apartment over the general store, which sat next door to our boardinghouse. My wife was busy preparing dinner for the boarders during the move-in, so I stood on sentry duty for her. My chief task was to call descriptions of the bachelor and his belongings to Judith while she finished the chores. In the lantern light, I saw that Mr. Vlach was indeed tall, dark, and handsome. His angular face was white as new milk, and he had a posh accent I couldn't place. Vlach was wiry and very strong, almost supernaturally so. I was amazed to see him shoulder crates that it had taken two hired men to lift off the wagon. I could never have handled a crate of that size without help.

When Mr. Vlach discovered that the hired men had removed the blankets from a six-foot-long box placed most carefully in the center of the wagon, he gave them a soft-voiced tongue lashing that made my ears ring. It seemed a harmless sort of blunder to cause such a ruckus. But the bachelor's rage was terrifying to behold. He loomed over the hired men, and they cowered away from him, almost gibbering in fear as they replaced the concealing blankets before carefully carrying the long box up the stairs to the apartment. I had only caught a brief glimpse of the box, but it chilled me to the bone. It was black as pitch and shaped like a coffin. My eyes burned red for several minutes after seeing it for the first time.

As soon as the last crate vanished upstairs into the apartment over the general store, I went to the kitchen to give her my final report. "I do not think I like our new neighbor," I said to Judith, parking myself in a chair at the kitchen table to keep out of her way as she cooked.

"Was he handsome?" she asked as she stirred the gravy.

"He was quite handsome. But he treated the hired men disrespectfully. He seems to have a bad temper. They uncovered a long box he had packed in the center of the wagon, and he gave them a tongue lashing right there in the middle of the street. It was . . . unkind."

I wanted to say more about the creepy coffin-shaped box, which had frightened me on a gut level, but I couldn't find the right words, so I settled for describing some of the furniture I'd seen instead.

After we cleaned up from supper, Judith and I went next door to welcome our new neighbor to town. Judith had baked her famous apple pie, and it smelled so good I rather hoped Mr. Vlach would ignore our knock on the door. But a moment later, it swung open with a strange hissing sound and the handsome man stood before us, his face pale in the flickering lamplight. We introduced ourselves and Judith handed him the welcome pie. He smiled seductively as he accepted the gift. "I am delighted to know that I have such kind and thoughtful neighbors," he purred, undressing my wife with his eyes. Judith blushed uncomfortably under his gaze.

"Anytime you need help getting something done, just let us know," I said, putting my arm possessively around Judith's waist. "Good evening to you." I hustled my wife off the porch and across the alley to our yard.

Judith giggled. "There's no need to be jealous, Jacob," she said. "He was just being friendly."

"Uh huh. And I'm the president of the United States," I said.

Judith gave me a humdinger of a kiss, which did a great deal to reassure me that I was the only fellow for her and coaxed me inside the house for a slice of the second pie that she'd stashed away in the cupboard as a surprise for me. I have an amazing wife.

The grand opening of the new general store was scheduled for twilight on a Thursday. The strange start time was a source of much speculation among the town gossips, until Mr. Vlach confided in the visiting minister that he had an intolerance to the sun, which too easily burned his pale skin. His physician encouraged him to work and socialize in the evening. After the grand opening, a hired boy would take care of his store during the day while he covered the night shift.

This explanation satisfied local curiosity, but also created a dilemma for those hosting Advent and Christmas celebrations in the afternoon. It created quite a hullabaloo, with daytime hostesses vying for the few open evenings left on the calendar. The land agent's wife nearly came to blows with the minister's spouse when she tried to reschedule her afternoon tea during the children's Christmas recital. Hastily updated invitations were sent around, noting that evening hours had been set aside for holiday celebrations so that our new neighbor could take part.

Thursday night rolled around, and the new general store opened its doors to the public. The whole town turned out to look the place (and its owner) over. Mr. Vlach was in evening clothes, which enhanced his handsome face and figure, and he quickly attracted a crowd of fluttering, blushing ladies who almost swooned when they heard his posh accent.

The general store had several luxury items as well as the plain fare offered by Vlach's predecessor. The ladies cooed and tutted over the lovely fabrics in one corner, and the gentlemen were grouped around the tobacco display, which stood beside the more common offerings of sugar, flour, and coffee. Then there were the ready-made items like shawls, table coverings, and both cotton and linen napkins. My wife, Judith, was agog over the offerings in the new store, moving from one area to the next, speechless in her excitement. By closing time, Vlach had sold almost everything on display, and he had been invited to every Advent and Christmas party in town.

Our paths crossed with Mr. Vlach on several occasions during his first week in town. He waltzed past us at the Christmas ball with the local schoolteacher mesmerized in his arms. Judith and I shared a table with him and the land agent's daughter during the annual Christmas tea. And I bid against him in the church's Christmas charity auction and lost, much to my chagrin. I'd wanted to give that handmade shawl to my wife for Christmas. Now I'd have to buy it from Mr. Vlach's store.

And speaking of the general store: I soon noticed that Mr. Vlach had a rather hypnotic effect on his customers. Whenever he appeared at the counter after dusk, folks bought twice as many items as they intended. It was rather creepy. Their eyes would glaze over, and any extras he suggested would be purchased without question. And his sway didn't end with the store. By the end of his second week in town, four different women had invited him to a private tête-à-tête over dinner at the local inn, which was very strange, considering all of them were happily married. Judith tutted over the situation, but what could you do? It was a free country, and if the local ladies wanted to make fools of themselves over a tall, dark stranger, that was their business—and their husbands'.

Mr. Vlach tried his hypnotism on me one evening when I went next door to buy some nails, but I was immune to those dark eyes with the red glint in their center. He looked rather chagrined that he couldn't persuade me to buy a very expensive and completely unnecessary plow for the farm-garden Judith kept behind the boardinghouse. "What do we need a plow for? It's December. The ground is frozen," I told Mr. Vlach crisply as I paid a few pennies for the nails. That was the last time I patronized his store, and I forbade Judith to step foot inside it. Better to shop in the next town than to put oneself voluntarily in the presence of Mr. Vlach.

Judith laughed at me, but she could tell I was truly worried about the man, so she promised to keep away. She had enough work to do cooking and cleaning up after the boarders. So that was all right.

During the second week of Advent, a new illness started spreading through town. It affected several of the local women. They turned pale and glassy-eyed, and red marks appeared on their throats or sometimes their wrists. The local doctor was baffled. He tried bleeding the disease out of their bodies, but that made things worse, so he stopped that technique and tried using elixirs to strengthen the blood. This seemed to offer the stricken some relief, but the disease continued to spread. The land agent's wife fell ill shortly after her Christmas tea. The local schoolteacher caught it next and had to cancel her classes. And the annual town Christmas dance was moved from the fancy ballroom in the Ingar mansion to the upstairs hall at the inn when Mistress Ingar contracted the disease.

I noticed that Mr. Vlach grew almost ruddy in appearance whenever someone in town fell ill. I also noticed that all the women who invited him to dinner had contracted the mysterious disease, as well as several debutantes who were in pursuit of the new bachelor. I grew suspicious and decided to discuss the situation with my Scottish grandmother, who was scheduled to visit us during the Christmas holidays. When I was a wee fellow, Granny had told me stories about evil creatures that only came out at night and drank the blood of humans, and I wondered if Mr. Vlach might be one of them.

I went to meet the stagecoach on the day Granny arrived. She practically sprang out of the door, and I wondered anew that she was still as spry as a spring chicken and more youthful at heart than many a schoolchild. We hugged and exclaimed over one another. I hired a local lad to cart her luggage across town to our boardinghouse and we strolled to the inn to have a cup of tea and catch up.

Over tea and cakes, I told Granny all about the new bachelor in town. Her face grew grim when I told her about the illness sweeping through the town and the symptoms exhibited by the afflicted. She tutted but didn't say much in such a public setting. It was only after we got home, and she and Judith had an enthusiastic reunion, that the two of us sat down together in her private sitting room and consulted an old tome she'd brought with her from the old country. Granny turned to the section entitled "On Dark and Foul Creatures" and read me the passage aloud. In summary, it said that there were evil creatures called *vampyren* or *revenants* that returned from the grave to prey upon the living. They slept during the day in coffins filled with the dirt from their grave and walked abroad at night. To stave off a return to death, they drank the blood of living humans. You could protect yourself against such beings by using garlic and holy objects, according to the book, but you could only kill them by plunging a wooden stake through their heart and removing their head.

"Sounds like your Mr. Vlach," Granny said, closing the book. I nodded grimly. So it did. I felt a sudden sense of urgency. I didn't like living in such close proximity to Mr. Vlach. The book said that vampires often killed their victims. I remembered Vlach's invasive perusal of my wife when we first met, and the thought terrified me.

I left on a business trip the day after Granny arrived. I was gone for two days, and barely made it home before dark on the third day. As I pulled to a stop outside the barn, our hired boy came running up.

"Oh, Mr. Porter, your wife is sick," he exclaimed. "She took sick last night, and the doctor thinks she's got the plague, same as the other folks in town."

I threw the reins to the hired boy and ran into the boardinghouse, heading for the rooms reserved for the family. Judith lay sleeping in bed, with Granny in a nearby chair, watching over her sleep. From the doorway I could see the red marks on her throat where Mr. Vlach had sucked her blood. I was filled with a blinding fury, and it took several moments to calm down.

I stepped to the side of the bed and tenderly stroked my sleeping wife's hair. Then I asked Granny what had happened. Apparently, the boardinghouse had run low on flour, so Judith went to the general store to buy more so she would have enough for breakfast in the morning. She was the only customer in the store at the time, and all she could remember was Mr. Vlach sweeping into the store from the back room to greet her with a dazzling smile. Then everything went blank. The next thing Judith recalled was stumbling dazedly into the kitchen with an aching neck and falling on the floor beside the sink. Granny sent immediately for the doctor, and then tucked Judith into bed with a great many cloves of garlic and a silver cross around her neck. The cross made Judith restless and upset, but Granny would not remove it.

Granny had assumed the upkeep of the boardinghouse with the assistance of several local women who went to our church. The ladies refused to be reimbursed, saying it was their Christian duty to help the sick, so she hadn't insisted.

I stared desperately at the marks on the neck of my sleeping wife. "What should I do, Granny? How do I defeat a . . . a creature like Mr. Vlach?"

Patting me comfortingly on the shoulder, Granny told me everything she'd been taught back in the old country. I took a steadying breath and nodded. I would do whatever it took to save my Judith.

While our boarders were eating the good dinner prepared by our church family, I went to the woodpile and started splitting logs and filing the pieces down into sharp stakes. I was going vampire hunting. If Granny's book was correct, the vampire might visit Judith again tonight. And I would be ready for him.

It was almost midnight when I heard the first hypnotic notes reverberate through our window. It sounded like someone was humming a high-pitched tune, and it had a startling effect on Judith. Her eyes popped open, and she sat bolt upright. Her gaze was misty and unseeing, yet she hopped out of bed with ease and floated gracefully across the floor. I followed her, wooden stake in one hand and mallet in the other. Judith swept quickly through the large kitchen and out the back door into the bitter December chill. The strange, almost-singing sound increased in intensity as Judith crossed the alley toward the general store. A dark figure in a sweeping black cloak was waiting at the back door. It turned its back to me as it swept Judith into its arms. It bent its head, sharp canines gleaming in the moonlight, and then recoiled when it saw Granny's silver cross around my wife's neck.

I took two silent steps forward and thrust the stake into the creature's heart with all my strength. It started bolt upright in pain, dropping Judith to the doorstep. I smashed the mallet against the stake, forcing it deeper into the vampire. Mr. Vlach gave a single, high-pitched whine like that of a wolf in pain and then collapsed, landing at the foot of the apartment staircase. I'd left an axe beside the woodpile just across the alley from the general store. I grabbed it and lopped off the vampire's head. There was no blood on the axe when I lifted it away from the body. I suppose Mr. Vlach had no blood of his own. Only that of his victims.

I carried Judith to our boardinghouse and tucked her back into bed with Granny to watch over her. Then I returned to the general store. I wrapped Mr. Vlach's head and body in thick blankets, carried him upstairs to his apartment, and placed him in the coffin that I found crouching menacingly in the bedroom. Using coals from the stove, I started a small fire inside the coffin and retreated silently to the boardinghouse. Granny and I watched from an upstairs window as the fire slowly burned through coffin and vampire. When the fire started spreading into the surrounding space, Granny raced downstairs to sound the alarm.

The entire town gathered to help contain the fire in the general store. The fire spread faster than I anticipated, as if it was trying to rid the world of the darkness that was Gelu Vlach. By the time a bucket brigade had formed, the entire building was encased. We evacuated the boardinghouse, which was the only building nearby, while several of the local fire watch tried in vain to reach the upstairs apartment to rescue Mr. Vlach. They were met with a wall of flames that was impossible to penetrate, and barely made it out in time before the roof collapsed. Fortunately, a dawn thunderstorm extinguished the fire before it spread to the boardinghouse. But the general store was completely gutted and all that remained of the town's most eligible bachelor were some burnt bones.

The ladies in town mourned the death of the suave bachelor, though I am not sure the same could be said of the cuckolded husbands. The local authorities searched for any records to tell them whom to notify of Mr. Vlach's death, but they found no family records, no heirs, and no moneybox. Mr. Vlach had paid cash for the general store and listed no next of kin on his bill of sale. In the end, Mr. Vlach was given a pauper's funeral three days before Christmas and his bones were buried in the church graveyard. I offered to pay for a tombstone, since I was his closest neighbor. The townsfolk thought I was being generous, but in truth, I wanted to make sure there was a very large stone cross standing over Vlach's grave, just in case.

The doctor was delighted when the strange illness quickly faded away, no doubt due to his healing elixirs. All the victims were better in time to attend the Christmas Eve service at the local church, where we celebrated the birth of our Lord and prayed for those in mourning for the departed Mr. Vlach. I was not one of the latter.

Wild Hunt

Our maternal grandmother lived in the White Mountains of New Hampshire, near the top of one of the highest peaks. It was a strange, magical place. When I was little, my parents would send my brother and I to stay with our grandmother for the summer. It was during these holidays that I discovered that elves and trolls and many other beings inhabited the forests and meadows. Any path you took could lead you to a small miracle—or a whole lot of trouble.

My grandmother told me not everyone could see the supernatural world, and I was not to speak of what I saw to anyone else. I didn't believe her. But then I tried discussing the magical creatures with some of the village children and they laughed at me. They called me "the girl who really believes in fairies." Their mockery stung, and I ran away to cry alone in my favorite spot by the stream. I spent the rest of that summer holiday playing with my younger brother and avoiding the neighborhood children. I never again spoke of the supernatural to the villagers. Lesson learned.

Two summers later, I was wandering the streets of the small town, watching the antics of several small fae who were playing

WILD HUNT

tag in and out of sunbeams, when an adorable puppy with a white blaze on its forehead trotted past me and turned into a crooked lane I had never seen before. It popped its little head around the corner and barked once at me, before disappearing back into the lane.

Curious, I followed the puppy through several twists and turns, until I came to a long wooden house that backed upon a dense forest. I'd never seen anywhere like it on the mountain. And the tall man in the sweeping hat and cloak who stood in the yard with his hand on the bridle of a splendid white horse was a stranger to me. I'd visited this village every summer since I was a babe, and thought I knew everyone in it. So this was a surprise.

The hat brim shadowed the man's face so I couldn't properly see his eyes as he looked me over. The puppy gamboled around him and then trotted back to dance around me.

"Do you like dogs, Leah?" the man asked.

I was surprised that he knew my name; but then again, he would have seen me every summer, even if I had never before noticed him.

"I do," I confirmed shyly. "But my new stepfather won't let me have one. He . . . he accidentally shot our father's hound last winter." I wasn't so sure it was an accident. Our stepfather had done everything he could to erase my papa's presence from our household, and killing his faithful hound seemed part and parcel of this initiative.

Something in my face and voice tipped the man off. His aura darkened. He replied: "I am sorry to hear that. My condolences on the loss of your father, and of his hound."

"Thank you," I said, fighting tears. I missed my papa terribly, and my mother had become a stranger since she married my stepfather.

"It is solstice, and I am hunting today," the man said. "This pup is too small to come with us. Would you watch over him until I return?"

My heart lifted and I felt a huge smile cross my face. "It would be my honor," I exclaimed.

He scooped up the puppy and placed him in my arms. Then he mounted his horse and gave a shrill whistle. At once, hunting hounds of all shapes and sizes came loping into the yard from the forest, yelping and baying and barking in delight. The whole yard was full of them. I couldn't get an accurate count, for they seemed to drift in and out of focus. The ones in the rear were so misty they might not have been real.

"Fare you well, Leah," the hunter called over the noise of the dogs. He flicked the reins, and his horse leapt into the air and galloped up into the sky, followed by a swarm of baying hounds.

The whole world seemed to whirl about me. When my head cleared, I was standing outside the confectioner's shop, holding a squirming puppy. I scratched the white blaze on his forehead and raced for my grandmother's house, not quite sure how to explain what had just happened to me. But explanations were unnecessary. Grandmother took one look at the pup in my arms and nodded in understanding. "Not everyone is trusted with such a task," she said. "Best make the pup a bed beside the fire. He will be with us for a while."

My little brother trotted in and exclaimed excitedly over the puppy. He had been devastated when Papa's hound died. The two were soon rolling on the floor while Grandmother and I started supper. Their antics kept us laughing all evening.

Late on the third night after the pup came to stay, I was awakened by a sound like a flock of geese flying over the house. Moments later, someone knocked on my grandmother's door. I slid down the ladder from the loft and glanced at my grandmother, who was standing by the fireplace.

"It is for you," she said.

I nodded and lifted the puppy from his basket. Then I opened the door, cradling the sleepy ball of fur in my arms. The hunter stood before me in his rough tunic and wide-brimmed hat. Behind him, the white horse nosed our patch of peppermint and the hounds sniffed and rolled and bumped one another in glee. As soon as the pup saw the hunter, he wiggled in delight until I could hardly hold him. I saw the hunter's flashing grin as he reached out and accepted the little dog from me.

"Thank you, Leah," he said.

A sob caught suddenly in my throat. "Thank you," I whispered, knowing he would understand what I meant. I missed my papa so much. I missed his faithful hound. I missed my former happy life. But I had no words to express all those feelings.

"We will meet again," the hunter said. His tone was so kind that I had to wipe tears from my eyes as he turned away and mounted the white horse. A moment later, hunter and hounds trotted into the sky, headed home.

It was traditional for our family to spend the twelve days of Christmas with our paternal grandmother in her mountain home, but this year my stepfather would not allow it. He had been glad to be rid of my brother and I for a whole summer when he and my mother first married, but his attitude changed when we returned for school in the fall, and he realized how useful we were around the house. Too useful, as it turned out. He dismissed the maid, groom, and cook that had served our family my whole life and assigned their tasks to myself and my brother. The workload was so difficult that we were rapidly falling behind in our studies at school. Worst of all, our mother did not protest or complain at this change in our household. It took me several weeks to realize that my mother was under some kind of spell, and the magician who cast it upon her was my new stepfather.

In my defense, I was so grief stricken after the death of my papa that I was in no condition to evaluate a potential enemy, particularly one that was sprung so suddenly upon us just a few meager months after our father passed away. If my stepfather was a magician, and if he'd put my mother under a spell, it would explain why she'd married him so suddenly after such a short acquaintance, and why she no longer seemed to care what happened to her children or the possessions of her first husband. A heart-thumping exploration of my stepfather's locked workshop—with my younger brother standing watch—quickly proved this theory but did not provide the means for remedying the situation. So, I wrote a letter to my grandmother, asking for her advice, and my brother smuggled it out to the post for me while he was out running errands.

On Christmas night, my stepfather and mother were relaxing in the parlor after dinner while my brother and I cleaned up when a loud honking and braying sound erupted over our community. My stepfather swore and leapt to his feet: "What in blazes is causing that noise? Can't a man enjoy his Christmas holiday in peace?"

My brother ran to the front door and flung it wide, looking up into the sky for the source of the sound. Suddenly, a large hound with a white blaze on his forehead trotted through the open portal, nudged me and my brother in a friendly manner, and went to lie down in the warmest spot beside the fire. My stepfather swore and shouted at the dog, then shouted at my brother.

"I don't know where he came from," my brother protested. "He just appeared on the porch when I opened the door."

The honking and braying sounds faded into the distance as my stepfather roared out his anger. By the time my mother interceded, the Wild Hunt was long gone. Calmly, she said: "Close the door, Leah, it is getting cold. Why don't you pour all of us some tea and cut more of the Christmas cake? A little refreshment will help us all feel better. Abe, go finish decorating the carriage. We will be making holiday calls over the next few days, and we want to look our best."

My brother and I obeyed her at once. It was the first time Mama had called either of us by name since we returned from our summer holiday. It was almost as if the presence of the dog had weakened the spell on her.

As we went about our assigned tasks, my stepfather tried to drag the hound out of the house. The dog refused to budge. I watched through the kitchen door as he tugged at the dog's neck and shoulders and legs. I was almost positive that the hound made himself heavier each time my stepfather pulled at him. There was a soft green glow at the edges of his fur, and a spark of red in his eyes.

My stepfather swore and picked up the fireplace poker. He tried to hit the dog with it, but somehow, he missed every time. The dog vanished and reappeared in an instant, a few inches away from the place where my stepfather was swatting.

"Give it up, George," my mother advised, not taking her eyes off her knitting. "It's Christmas. Someone gave us a new dog, and it would behoove us to accept the gift with grace."

My stepfather stomped over to his chair and sat down with a bang. I quickly brought in a tray with the Christmas cake and passed refreshments to my mother and stepfather. When my stepfather's face was safely behind the newspaper, I rubbed my pup on his blaze and gave him a piece of Christmas cake. "Good boy," I whispered.

Over the next few days, my stepfather did his best to get rid of our new hound. On St. Stephen's Day, he tried to run the beast over with the carriage while we made holiday calls on our friends and neighbors. On the Feast of St. John, his gun "accidently" went off in the direction of the dog while he was cleaning it in the garden shed. Instead of wounding the dog, the bullet killed the prize rooster my stepfather had purchased to improve the quality of his livestock. On New Year's Eve, my stepfather knocked the dog into the well and slammed down the lid. As he turned away in triumph, the dog appeared right in front of him and shook himself, showering my stepfather with cold water. On the feast of St. Basil the Great, my stepfather put a rope around the dog's neck, hoping to throttle him. Instead, the beast used the rope to drag my stepfather through every mudpuddle and dirty snowbank in the yard, before depositing him into the manure pile at the back of the barn.

As the twelve days of Christmas progressed, my mother slowly returned to normal. Her moments of lucidity were more frequent, her forgiving attitude toward my stepfather waned, and her remarks became pointed and much drier.

After dinner on Epiphany, Mama appeared in the kitchen and asked me if the cook was on holiday.

"No, Mama, stepfather fired her in September, remember?" I replied, scrubbing industriously at a dirty pot so I wouldn't have to see the look on her face.

"I do not remember," Mama said, her voice strained. "I seem to have forgotten a lot of things lately. Who has been doing all the cooking since then?"

"I have, Mama," I said, carefully drying the pot with a cloth.

"That's what I thought," she said grimly.

Our hound appeared in the kitchen door. He nosed Mama's hand as she marched past him and out the door. Then he came over and sat on my foot.

"Here you go, my cheeky beggar," I said, feeding him a meat roll and rubbing the blaze on his forehead. He swallowed it whole, reared up to lick my cheek, then nudged open the back door with his nose and trotted outside to beg for a second snack from my gullible brother, who was chopping wood.

A moment later, I heard Mama shouting in the barn. I couldn't make out the words, but I knew from her tone that someone was in trouble. I threw down my dishcloth and ran as fast as I could toward the sound. My brother raced over from the woodpile, and together we burst into the barn to see what was going on.

Mama and our stepfather were shouting at one another in the center aisle.

"You fired my servants and enslaved my children because you *love* me?" Mama roared. "That's not love. That's selfishness and greed and . . . and . . . lust!"

"Shut your mouth, woman," shouted my stepfather. He pulled a wand out of his pocket and pointed it at her. Suddenly my mother could no longer speak. Her lips moved, but no sound came out.

"As for you brats, I've had enough of you too," he cried, aiming his wand at us. I gasped and threw myself in front of my younger brother, trying to protect him from whatever spell our evil stepfather wanted to put on us. At the same moment, I saw the star-blaze hound trot through the back door of the barn. With each step, he was gaining height and bulk until he was larger than my stepfather's prized horses. As my stepfather uttered the first words of his spell, the enormous hound swatted him to the floor with one paw and then sat down on his sprawled figure.

The spell on my mother broke at once. She gasped for breath and then grabbed us in her arms. I pulled away just long enough to seize my stepfather's wand so he couldn't use it against us.

Above our heads, I heard baying and yipping sounds, as if a thousand geese were migrating overhead. Suddenly, the barn was swarming from end-to-end with enormous, red-eyed hunting hounds. It was Twelfth Night, and the Wild Hunt had arrived, just in time.

The milling dogs parted to allow a white horse and his rider to trot through the double doors. When the hunter saw the star-blazed hound sitting on my stepfather, he smiled.

"Well done," he said.

The star-blazed hound stood up and picked up my stepfather by the back of his shirt, scruffing him as if he were a naughty puppy.

"You won't get away with this," my stepfather howled, glaring at the hunter.

"Your time is up," the hunter replied coldly. "You have forfeited your life *and* your eternity. From now on, you will hunt with me."

Before our eyes, my stepfather shrank rapidly, transforming into a red-eyed puppy with a wand-shaped marking across his little shoulders. The tiny pup yapped at the hunter, then crouched down to widdle on the floor.

"Come. We must circle the whole world before dawn." The hunter blew his horn to indicate they were moving off. The hounds bayed and streamed out of our barn, trotting quickly up into the sky, the new puppy in their midst. My star-blazed hound wagged his entire back end in excitement. He licked each of us before following his master on the white horse.

"Your hound will be back tomorrow, Leah," the Master of the Wild Hunt called to me, "And I will see you next summer."

Then he galloped his white steed up into the sky, sounding the hunting horn once more as the Wild Hunt set off on their annual Twelfth Night ride to punish evildoers and gather up the dead.

22

The Dollar

Priscilla cuddled the baby in her lap and smiled at her cousin-in-law. "A Christmas werewolf! The first Dubois child born during the twelve days of Christmas in a century. Well done, Evangeline."

Evangeline beamed. "We had no idea she would be born during the Season of the Wolf. She wasn't due to arrive until the middle of January. But the little miss surprised us!"

Loup-garou born during the Season of the Wolf had special gifts. They often became skilled diplomats who led the family to new heights in business, society, health, politics, and more. They were devoted to the good of the community.

"If she is anything like her great-grandfather, we can expect great things. Werewolf, healer, diplomat, and more," Jean-Claude said suavely, removing the baby from his wife's arms to drop a kiss on her dainty forehead. "Welcome to the family, my dear. I am your new god-papa."

The baby blinked and her nose twitched. Her senses were already enhanced, and she got a good whiff of her godfather while he walked through the rented hall, showing off the new addition to the assembled throng. Tomorrow, they would attend

The Dollar

her New Year's Day christening. Tonight, the extended Dubois family and their friends celebrated their Christmas miracle with a ball, prepared to dance the evening away.

After Jean-Claude delivered his tiny darling back to her mother, he sought out the only other Christmas *loup-garou* currently gracing the family. Jules had passed the century mark two years ago but was still lean and spry. And as dedicated to his home, his family, and his community as ever. He stood in a hidden corner, watching one of the departing guests with a frown.

"What troubles you, *mon oncle?*" Jean-Claude asked softly.

Jules turned, and Jean-Claude was surprised by the tears in his ancient blue eyes. "I am old, my nephew, and I mourn for this town in which I was born. It was once a good community, but the blessing departed from this place long ago. We will be moving soon; Evangeline, Henri, the babe and me, for we cannot raise our Christmas werewolf in this evil place."

Jean-Claude was shocked. He thought nothing would ever remove Jules and his family from this town where their ancestors settled more than two hundred years before.

"It pains me to see a problem so long unsolved," Jules continued. "I fear it will continue to impact the good folk of this town long after I am gone."

"Tell me of this problem," Jean-Claude invited, waving a hand to the comfortable chairs in the hidden nook. "Perhaps I can help." As head of the Dubois werewolf clan, it was his duty to help his great-uncle if help were possible.

"The man who just left the party, he is a bad man, *neveu*," Jules said, accepting a glass of champagne from a passing server. "He is the mayor of our small town and owns the local bank too. I have watched his evil ways from afar and have done what I can to shield the community from his wickedness, but he is clever and has many dangerous connections."

"Too vague, *oncle*," Jean-Claude said, taking a sip of champagne. "Give me specifics."

"Extortion. Blackmail. Misappropriation of community funds. Some say he has even resorted to murder."

"Against the family?" Jean-Claude asked sharply. Something like this should have been brought to his attention long ago.

"*Non, mon neveu*," Jules replied. "He has done much evil in this community, but he takes care not to infringe upon our family, so I have never had reason to take steps against him. He is very careful, this man. His crimes are blamed upon others, and those that cannot be bribed or blackmailed into supporting his initiatives end up dead."

"Still too vague," Jean-Claude said. "Perhaps a story to enlighten me?"

Jules set down his drink. "For too long, I have guarded my tongue to protect our family from this man. The truth no longer comes easily to me. But, as you say, a story may suffice."

He leaned back and gazed out the window into the snowy night. As the minutes ticked slowly toward midnight, Jules told the story of two sisters who had lived their whole lives in this town.

The story began with Jean, who was the quiet and plain daughter of the local banker. She was swept off her feet by the up-and-coming young mayor, who married her because he wanted to become a partner in her father's bank. His goal was swiftly achieved after the vows were exchanged. Their marriage was not a happy one. It soon became apparent that Jean could not conceive the mayor's long-coveted child, and before long, his eye started roving. When a wealthy beauty moved into town, the mayor decided she was a much better match for him than the banker's plain daughter.

When Jean suddenly perished due to blood loss from an apparent miscarriage, the whole town turned out for the funeral. Later that evening, Jean's maid came privately to her family and told them the truth. Jean had been stabbed to death during an argument with her husband, and the local doctor had been bribed with a handsome sum to sign off on her cause of death. Before the family could initiate an investigation, the lady's maid was discovered hanging from the rafters of the mayor's barn with a suicide note pinned to her collar. In it, she claimed responsibility for her mistress's murdering, saying Jean had caught her stealing an expensive necklace.

The family knew the note was fake because the lady's maid, who had served them before accompanying Jean to her new home, could neither read nor write. But the local authorities refused to listen to them. They accepted the suicide note at face value and closed both cases. So the matter was settled in the mayor's favor. Three months later, he married the wealthy beauty.

Celia's society debut took place a year after her sister Jean's death. She married a rising young lawyer and they soon took their place in local society. Their only son was born the same year as the mayor's only son. The two boys were rivals from the start: in school, in sports, in entertaining. The lawyer was a wealthy man and did what he could to protect people from the increasing predations of their corrupt political system. This infuriated the mayor, but the lawyer had powerful connections that kept him in check. For almost two decades, the two community leaders maintained an uneasy truce, even when it came to the intense rivalry between their sons.

Things came to a head just before Christmas this year, when a complaint was lodged against the bank, which prompted an audit. It was quickly discovered that someone at the bank was misappropriating funds, and suspicion fell on both the mayor and his former father-in-law, who co-owned the bank.

Celia's father proclaimed his innocence and hired his son-in-law to investigate the matter. A week later, the banker was found hanging from the roof of his office with a note confessing to the crime. Once again, the local authorities accepted the suicide note as true and tried to close the case. But Celia's husband knew his father-in-law had been murdered and threatened to sue the town government if the case did not remain open.

While her husband argued with the sheriff's office and city hall, Celia worked diligently with the family accountant, searching the books for proof of her father's innocence. Then a note arrived from her aunt in Baton Rouge, who was caring for her grief-stricken mother. The message said Celia's mother had taken a turn for the worse and she must come immediately to say her farewell. Celia dropped everything and boarded the next train. When she arrived, she found her mother sipping tea in the kitchen. She was pale and wan, but there was no sign of a life-threatening illness in her countenance, only surprise and pleasure at her daughter's unexpected visit.

Celia's mother and aunt were alarmed when they learned that a false note was the cause of her visit. They begged Celia to return home at once. Someone had gone to a great deal of trouble to get her out of the way. She might foil their scheme if she returned early. Celia went at once to the train station to purchase a return ticket, not even pausing for a meal. Her stomach was roiling with dread, and she did not think it wise to eat.

As soon as she arrived at her home station, Celia knew it was too late. The sheriff was waiting for her on the platform, expression solemn and hat in hand. He sadly informed her that her son and husband had a terrible quarrel shortly after she left for Baton Rouge, and the boy had shot his father and then himself.

"The sheriff believed this story, after everything else that had happened between this family and the mayor?" asked Jean-Claude skeptically.

"The sheriff has long been a creature of the mayor," Jules replied.

Jean-Claude leaned back in his chair and closed his eyes, not wanting to ask his next question. "And this is just one terrible story among many?" he queried.

"Just one story among many," Jules confirmed. The elderly Christmas werewolf sighed. His special gifts had always centered around protecting the family and enhancing the community in which they lived. Making lives better. This situation weighed heavily upon him.

"I understand why you are leaving this place," Jean-Claude said at last. "Find a new home where *la belle petite fille* can grow and thrive in peace. As for the rest, let me see what I can do."

His eyes were fixed on a sad-eyed woman in black who was speaking with Priscilla and Evangeline. He moved without haste across the crowded ballroom and caught the last words of their conversation. "I cannot stay, Evangeline. It is inappropriate to celebrate in my mourning year. But I did want to stop for a moment to thank you for everything you've done for us through the years and wish you farewell. I will be leaving on the morning train."

"I am so sorry for your loss, Celia," Evangeline whispered, tears in her lovely eyes.

"I am so happy for your gain, Evangeline," the lady in black replied. She dropped a kiss on her friend's cheek, caressed the baby's cheek with one finger, and disappeared through a side door into the snowy darkness.

"My darling," Jean-Claude whispered in his wife's ear. "I have an errand to run. If I am not back by midnight, I will give you a dozen kisses to make up for my neglect."

"If you can do anything to help that woman, I will forgo the dozen kisses and the neglect," Priscilla replied. "Her pain feels familiar to me. I know what it is to be the victim of cruelty."

Jean-Claude pressed a comforting hand against her shoulder and then followed Celia into the frosty night. It did not take him long to find her, for she had merely crossed the street to kneel at the altar in the cathedral, which was already set up for the New Year's Day christening ceremony.

Jean-Claude bowed to the altar and then knelt beside her.

"Why do you weep, lady?"

Celia started, for his approach had been silent. Turning teary eyes upon him, she said: "I weep for those whom I have lost this season, and those whom I lost long ago."

"A husband and a child, I think," the werewolf said. "A sister and a father."

"You know my story, then," Celia replied, crossing herself and rising to take a seat in the first pew.

"I have heard rumors," he replied, echoing her gestures, and sitting in the pew just behind her.

"Did the rumors tell you that the bank has foreclosed on my house, demanding immediate payment though we did not miss a single bill? Did they tell you that my husband's will states that all his money goes to the mayor's favorite 'charity' instead of his wife?" Celia asked. She reached into the small purse at her side and withdrew a bill. "When I put this dollar into the offering box, I will not have a penny left to my name. Evangeline and her husband, they were the ones who bought me a train ticket so that I can go home to my family. They insist it is not charity because I am a friend. But we all know it is charity."

"It is a good time of year to care for one's family and friends," Jean-Claude said. "But I have a better use for that dollar, friend of my cousin."

She turned in the pew to meet his gaze. "What use, cousin of my friend?"

"There is a small branch in our family tree that engages in a time-honored business; and has done so for several hundred years," Jean-Claude replied.

"And that business is?" the woman prompted when he paused.

"Assassination," Jean-Claude purred. "And because it is New Year's Eve, and in celebration of the birth of our tiny Christmas angel, the current going rate for an assassination is . . . one dollar."

***

Jean-Claude and Priscilla celebrated Epiphany in New Orleans; feasting with those members of the clan who lived locally. The next morning, their cousin passed along a letter from Evangeline.

"Oh, how terrible," Priscilla said as she read the missive over breakfast. "According to Evangeline, the mayor of their town perished tragically on New Year's Day. He and several of his business associates attended an afternoon deer hunt and were savaged by a pack of hungry wolves. Not one of them survived the encounter."

"A tragedy indeed," agreed Jean-Claude, pouring himself another cup of coffee.

"The town sent hunters out to kill the pack, but so far they haven't had much luck."

"Wolves have a very large territory," Jean-Claude said. "The pack may have moved on to a location with more plentiful game."

"I'm sure that is the case," Priscilla said.

They shared a smile across the table.

"In other news," Priscilla continued. "Evangeline's friend Celia—the one who lost her husband and son so tragically—has arrived safely in Baton Rouge and is now living with her mother and aunt. We should pay a call on them before we return home, my darling."

"We should," he agreed. "And I think we should bring Anton with us. He can look after the widow and her family when we are gone."

"Antoinette's brother? The bachelor?" Priscilla asked.

"The very one," Jean-Claude said happily. "It would be good for the lovely Celia and her mother to have a werewolf in the family, *oui*?"

23

Kobold Toymaker

I was eight years old when we left *Köln* in what is present-day Germany to come to Wisconsin. *Mein Vater,* he came from a noble family and was expected to follow in his father's footsteps. But his father was stern and cruel, and they could never agree. After one particularly fierce argument with his parents, Vater sold everything we had, packed up the family, and left on the first boat he could find for America. We had kinfolk in Wisconsin who would help us make a new start.

The ocean journey took more than a month. I was seasick at first, and homesick for my pretty house and my dolls, but we were no longer a noble family, *Mein Vater* told me. We were Americans now, and we could not afford to have pretty things until we earned them for ourselves. But my three brothers and I soon made friends with the other children on board, and when the weather was fair, we would laugh and play together while our parents visited with other families on deck. Sometimes they would make music and we would all dance.

I didn't like the stormy days in the hold of the ship, with everyone packed together like sardines in a tin. And some of the children got sick. Mama kept us away from the sick ones,

KOBOLD TOYMAKER

fearing we would become ill. But my five-year-old brother got measles—he was the only one of us who had not had them before we left Köln. He died on that voyage, as did twelve other children. It was a very sad beginning to our new life in America.

Mein Vater knew precisely what to do when we got to New York, for his cousin had written him a letter telling him how to get to Wisconsin. We hurried past the men trying to sell us things we did not need—*con men*, Vater called them—and went to the office of a steamboat to book passage up the Hudson River, through the Erie Canal, and onto a ship that would take us across the Great Lakes to Milwaukee. The trip took us ten days.

The cousin of *mein Vater* met us in Milwaukee and took us to his farm. The money Vater had made selling our possessions was enough to buy us land, and we stayed with our cousins while the other German men in our settlement erected a small farmhouse and a barn for us. We loved our new home, my brothers and me. We had lived in the city all our lives, and so life on a farm was very new and very wonderful to us.

Most of Vater's money had gone into the purchase of the land and the equipment needed to farm it. We had little left over for the luxuries that we'd left behind. But we took delight in the two cows and the hens given to us by our cousin, and we explored the woods surrounding our wheat fields when the chores were done. We learned to milk and gather eggs. Mama, who had never worked a day in her life, learned to churn butter and cook and make a garden, with the help of her new friends from the Lutheran church in town. Her soft white hands grew brown and calloused, but she was still the same sweet Mama, and she never complained of her loss of status or of the labor she now endured for the sake of Vater's dream.

Vater grew wheat, like our cousin. In the fall, a machine went from farm to farm to help thresh the farmers' wheat. Mama cooked up a great feast for all the men who came to help Vater when it was our turn to use the threshing machine.

We had enough food for winter, and warm—if plain— clothes to wear. But the crop our first year was small. Vater would have to cut down many more trees to have large wheat fields like those of his cousins. He would cut down the trees during the winter and sell the lumber at the local sawmill, and in spring we would all help root out the stumps to make a new field for Vater's wheat.

We settled down for a long, cold winter with much help from the cousins. We really knew so little about living off the land that first year. Mama announced early in November that there would be no presents this year for Saint Nicholas Day. Every penny had gone into buying coal and flour and other supplies for the long winter. But she would prepare a big dinner for us to eat and be merry with, and perhaps Vater would earn enough next year for us to exchange gifts.

Of the many shocks my brothers and I had received during that year of transition to a new life, this was the worst. We had always had elaborate celebrations for Saint Nicholas Day back at home. Parades and feasts, visits from Krampus to make sure we had been good children all year, and on the night of December 5, we would put our shoes by the front door. In the morning, our shoes would be filled up with fruits and nuts, and many gifts would surround each one. Mostly the gifts were from Mama and Vater, but I had always believed a few were from Saint Nicholas himself or one of his kobold toymakers.

Mama put on a brave face for us when she talked about Saint Nicholas Day, but we knew—my brothers and I—that she was ashamed to be so poor that she had nothing to give her children. Not even a few pennies left over for store-bought candy. That first year on the frontier, she knew none of the little tricks that the other farm wives used to make toys and candy from what little they had. She'd had enough difficulty just learning the things she must in order for us to survive.

My brothers and I decided to make gifts for one another, and we went searching around the barn and the woods and the house for leftover bits and pieces to use in their construction. During the summer I had grown out of the last of my pretty clothes from my old life, and they had been packed away at the bottom of my little trunk. I dug out a white linen frock and a thick velvet one and took them up to the garret with my little scissors and my sewing kit to try to come up with something creative to make for my family.

As I sat staring at the pretty fabrics, I heard a small tap-tap-tapping sound coming from the far corner. I looked around, and there was a tiny little man in a close-fitting brown jacket with a cap—what we call a *zipfelkappen*—on top of his tiny head. There was a tassel on the end of it, and the little nose above his long white beard was shiny red at the tip. He sat on a small stool, tapping away at a long leather object he held in his hands. It looked like a new shoe, just the size for Frederick, my eldest brother. The shoes he brought from our old home were too small now and had holes in them.

I stared at the little man with my mouth hanging open in surprise. It was a kobold toymaker. One of Saint Nicholas's helpers— at least, that was the story my nanny told me back in Köln.

"Mind your manners, *Mädchen*," he said gruffly when he noticed my staring. "If you are going to share the garret with me, then do so quietly. I have much work to do before the Feast."

I nodded, unable to speak, and turned back to my sewing. I decided to make handkerchiefs for my brothers and father, fashioned from the too-small white linen dress, and a pretty collar for my mother, made from the blue velvet. I set to work, staying near the window to make the most of the winter sunlight. On the other side of the garret, the tap-tapping sound changed. I glanced over and saw that the toymaker was carving something from a slab of wood. It looked like a wooden train for my middle brother, Klaus, to play with.

When the light faded, I went downstairs to help Mama with supper. I didn't mention the kobold. My parents and Frederick didn't believe in fairy tales. When Klaus and I were doing the dishes, I told him what I had seen in the garret. His eyes popped out in amazement, and when the last dish was dried, we crept upstairs and peeked inside. From the far corner, there came a tap-tap-tapping sound, and we saw the little kobold working by the light of a tiny candle.

"Nosy children will get coal in their shoes," he snapped, without turning his head from his task. Giggling in amazement, we scurried away.

Vater and Mama looked up from their reading as we settled down to study near the warm stove. They smiled at our bright faces and listened to us recite our lessons. It was three days until Saint Nicholas Day and suddenly, I couldn't wait!

I spent every spare minute working on the handkerchiefs and velvet collar, but I didn't return to the garret for fear the kobold would leave without finishing his Saint Nicholas Day gifts. I had brought some embroidery thread with me from our old home, and so I made a fancy blue edging for each handkerchief and put my father's initials on one of them, and Frederick's and Klaus's initials on the others. Then I sewed up the pretty velvet collar for Mama, and my gifts were done.

After Mama and I had finished making breads and puddings and pies for the Saint Nicholas feast, and after our parents had gone to bed on December 5, my brothers and I gathered up all the shoes and put them by the front door. We laid out our presents, telling each other over and over not to peek, and then hurried off to bed. Klaus and I exchanged excited grins as we parted for the night.

The next morning, Vater was the first one up. His exclamation of surprise woke everyone in the house, and we all hurried to the front room, wild with excitement. There were

Vater's work boots, filled with dried fruit and nuts and candy from the kobold. Beside the boots were several gifts, including my handkerchief, a carved bear from Frederick, a strange contraption that was for cleaning boots from Klaus, and a new leather harness for the horses, which could only have come from the kobold. Vater stared and stared at the new leather harness that he needed so badly, for he had only been able to afford a worn-out secondhand harness when we arrived.

Mother's shoes were also filled with good things to eat, and beside them were the velvet collar, a pretty wood carving of a rabbit from Frederick, a strange contraption for cleaning the stove from Klaus, and a pile of beautiful pink lawn fabric from the kobold.

Next to the boys' shoes were the handkerchiefs and some strange-looking toys they'd invented for themselves. The kobold had left Frederick the new shoes and Klaus a beautifully carved and painted wooden train with wheels that really moved.

By my shoes were a handkerchief box carved by Frederick and a device for storing thread made by Klaus. That was all. No toys from the kobold. The place where my shoes stood looked very bare compared to the rest.

Then we heard a thump, thump, thump as heavy footsteps came down the stairs from the garret. The kobold came into the front room carrying a huge dollhouse with fancy turrets and many windows, and little shingles on the roof. Everyone stared at him in shock as he trudged over and laid the dollhouse at my feet.

"For a good *Mädchen* on Saint Nicholas Day," he said to me. Then he nodded to my parents, winked at my brothers, and disappeared in a puff of air. My parents exclaimed in surprise and delight, and everyone clustered around, admiring their gifts, until Vater shooed us off to do our chores and Mama went to cook our feast.

It was the very best Saint Nicholas Day we had ever had. In later years, we became prosperous, and the gifts we exchanged were store bought. We never received kobold gifts again. Just that one special year, when we had nothing to give each other but love and the things we could make with our own hands.

24

Gingerbread House

BLOOMINGTON, MINNESOTA

It was Christmas season, and little kids were disappearing from the mall. It was terrible and frightening, and as of this morning, it was my problem. The chief phoned before I was properly out of bed and turned the matter of the missing children over to me and my partner. The senior (and more incompetent) detective team had been bumbling around for weeks since the first child went missing. They had finally been removed from the case last night when a third child vanished. Maybe the district would come to its sense at last and fire them. One could hope.

The biggest mystery wasn't why, but *how*. We assumed someone was kidnapping the children, but we couldn't figure out how. The method was a mystery. All of the entrances, exits, and staff hallways had security cameras on them. And none of the security cameras showed the children leaving the mall, alone or with an adult. We had hours of video from various cameras giving us glimpses of each child entering the property with their families, shopping at various stores, eating in the food court, and visiting Santa in his workshop. But nowhere existed footage of them exiting the mall. We couldn't even be sure if they were

194

GINGERBREAD HOUSE

kidnapped, or had fallen victim to a strange accident, a hitherto unknown danger in the structure of the mall.

To further complicate matters, in all three cases the families had split up the group so the various siblings could keep their Christmas gifts secret from one another. None of the families could pinpoint an exact time or place when their child went missing, because each assumed the child was shopping with the other parent.

I poured coffee into a travel mug and frowned as I looked for my backpack. My family had the second sight going way back in history, and gifted members like me always carried some kind of bag with an assortment of items that their gift told them might come in useful for the day. My sixth sense kept sending me a picture of the rope I used for rock climbing on the weekends. I had no idea why I'd need rope when I would be spending the day investigating at the mall. But I didn't question my sixth sense, I just dug the rope out of the closet, put it into my backpack, and headed downtown to meet my partner near Santa's Workshop in the northern section of the mall.

It was still early, and the mall hadn't opened for business when I arrived. My partner, Fred Mulligan, was already there with the manager, sipping his first cup of coffee for the day. He grinned when he saw my backpack. We'd worked together long enough that he knew all about my sixth sense. "Got everything you need in there?" he teased. There was an underlying note of respect in his tone, for I was not often wrong. "I think so," I replied, just as the mall manager arrived to escort us inside the building.

The place was massive, but fortunately for us, all three families had followed a similar pattern during their visit: eating at the food court at the southern end of the mall and visiting Santa's Workshop at the northern end. We would focus our attention on these two sections. Our first priority was to figure out how the children had vanished without being seen on the security cameras. So Mulligan headed to the south end of the mall to search for clues in the food court, while I concentrated my efforts on the Christmas display in the north.

Santa's Workshop was a Christmas wonderland, decorated from floor to ceiling with evergreen and holly, giant wrapped packages, several huge Christmas trees, miniature railroads, Santa's grotto with its old-time cottage walls and roof, and a raised platform where Santa's chair was enthroned between two Christmas trees full of presents. Directly opposite Santa's grotto was a massive Gingerbread House that dominated the entire wall. It reminded me at once of the story of Hansel and Gretel. Every kind of luscious candy was represented, from chocolate bar doors to candy cane pillars that stretched from floor to ceiling. The fake gingerbread walls were massive, the windows and doors decorated with colorful candy pieces. The roof looked like it was lined with black licorice, and the chimney was a molded slab of red velvet cake and white frosting formed into bricks. There were sliding boards, tunnels, nets to walk on, towers to climb.

I started searching for clues in the grotto, since all three of the missing kids had their pictures taken with Santa. I examined the security cameras, exit and ingress points, places where small children might hide from a hovering parent. I even tapped the walls, looking for a concealed door or staff exit that wasn't in view of the security cameras. Nothing.

I worked slowly and patiently through Santa's Workshop and the miniature railroad displays. I didn't want carelessness to cause me to miss a vital clue. But my gaze kept returning to the Gingerbread House. It was on the far wall, nowhere near the single exit. Even if the children had hidden in the crawl spaces or towers, they would have had to walk across the floor and exit through the front doors of the Christmas display, in full view of the cameras. It was clearly impossible for them to have been taken from the Gingerbread House. But my sixth sense kept nudging me in that direction.

I searched the Gingerbread House as carefully as the grotto. There were rooms full of interactive toys and games in Christmas and candy themes. There were spiral staircases leading to candy towers, connected by chocolate walkways and pink nets that resembled stretch taffy for the children to climb on. Candy stick sliding boards and rock candy climbing walls; lollypop ladders and butterscotch disc swings. It was a kid's paradise.

I was crawling through one of the entry tunnels on the far-right side of the Gingerbread House when my hand accidentally landed on a round peppermint candy embedded unexpectedly in the plastic gingerbread wall. At my touch, the wall opened. I found myself looking down a side tunnel that pierced through the wall of Santa's Workshop and sloped downward almost immediately. A secret door leading to a secret tunnel. I was pretty sure I had my answer.

I called Mulligan at once and told him what I'd found. "I'm going in. The kids may be trapped in here."

"Keep your radio on, just in case. I'll be there as soon as I can," he said.

"I'm going to tie a rope to the candy cane pillar and bring it down with me," I said. "There must be some reason the kids didn't come back up. Maybe the floor gave way. If that's what happened, I can climb down and search for them."

"So that's what you put in your backpack! Your sixth sense strikes again," Mulligan said. "Be careful."

I kept the channel on as I tied the rope to the pillar and then started down the hidden tunnel, playing out the rope as I went. Suddenly, I ran out of floor and plunged down a hidden slide. I gasped and tightened my grip on the rope to stop myself. I heard Mulligan call out to me over the radio, but his voice faded to static before I could respond. Then the radio went dead. Should I go back, or move on? I elected to move on.

I began inching myself down the slide, keeping the rope taut. The slow progress allowed me to get a better sense of my surroundings. And they were . . . strange. The walls were misty and seemed to swirl at the corner of my eyes. Funny flickering lights appeared and disappeared at intervals as I descended. I had the strange feeling that I was traveling back in time.

When my feet hit the floor at the bottom of the slide, I stood up. The strange mist surrounded me completely. I glanced behind and found that the slide had vanished from my sight. The only sign of the upper world was my rope, disappearing upward into the gray swirls. I gulped and clutched it tighter, remembering that Hansel and Gretel lost their way because their breadcrumbs were eaten. I didn't want to get stuck underneath a Gingerbread House like the children in the fairy tale.

There was a faint light ahead of me. I stepped toward it through the gray mist, letting out more of the rope as I walked.

When the swirls cleared, I found myself in a witch's house. I had no other words to describe it. It looked like a movie set, except this was the real deal. The cottage walls were made of crumbling brown stuff that looked and smelled like gingerbread. The door on the right was a slab of yellow-striped hard candy. The window on the left, which overlooked a wood filled with massive trees, was framed by boiled sweets. The smell of sugar and honey and molasses and maple syrup made my nose twitch. It was overwhelmingly . . . cloyingly . . . sweet. In front of me was a huge fireplace with a black cauldron bubbling over an open fire. On either side of the fireplace were shelves filled with strange, pickled creatures in jars, beakers of chemicals and brews, and magical-looking books.

A large table sat against the wall to the left, under the window. It had cooking pots, sharp knives, and herbs scattered across its surface. Suspended over the table were three wooden cages that hung from the rafters. Their doors were tied with heavy ropes. Inside each cage was a missing child. I recognized all three immediately from their photos and the footage I'd seen from the security cameras.

My first priority was to rescue the kids. We were alone in the room, at least for now, and I needed to release them before their captor returned. The children were fast asleep, and my heart sank with dread. It would be much harder to get them out of the cages and back up the slide if they were drugged. But I'd carry them out on my back if I had to.

I reeled out more of the rope, but quickly realized I would need both hands to get the children out of the cages, so I tied it around my waist. Then I grabbed the largest knife from the table, climbed on one of the chairs, and started cutting through the knots on the closest cage. I worked quickly and quietly, but the swaying of the cage woke the child, a black-haired five-year-old boy. He stared at me with frightened eyes, then relaxed when he realized I wasn't his captor.

"I'm here to rescue you," I whispered. "I'm Detective Martin, a police officer in your town. I'm going to take you back to your mom and dad. But you must be very quiet and do exactly as I say." The little boy nodded to show he understood. I carefully opened the door to the cage and lifted him out. Then I set him on the floor and said: "Take hold of the rope and follow it into the mist. Use it to climb up the sliding board and back down the tunnel. My partner, Detective Mulligan is waiting outside the Gingerbread House to take you to the police station so we can call your parents."

The little boy grabbed the rope with both hands and trotted toward the mist. A moment later, the tug around my waist indicated he was climbing up the slide.

The other children had awakened when I was rescuing the first boy. I held my finger to my lips, and they nodded, too frightened of their captor to make a noise. I cut open the second cage and released a six-year-old red-haired girl, who grabbed hold of the rope and hurried after the first boy.

I was just lifting the third boy down when the yellow-striped candy door banged open and a woman in a witch's costume entered the room.

"Run," I shouted to the boy, setting him on the floor and reaching for my gun. The boy wasted no time. He grabbed the rope and ran as fast as he could for the misty doorway and safety.

"You released my dinner," screeched the wild figure in the doorway when she saw the child escaping.

"You are under arrest," I shouted back, trying to distract her from the boy. The witch turned her glare on me. I was still standing on top of the chair, an easy target, I realized as she pulled out a crooked wand and shot a blue bolt of magical fire in my direction. I dove off the chair and rolled under the table, firing a shot of my own. But she was already moving, shooting magical blue bursts at me. I kept moving myself, rolling to avoid the shots and trying to maneuver behind a sturdy object so I could shoot back. But I got tangled up in my rope and was forced to roll in the opposite direction, so I didn't tie myself up.

The witch took advantage of my momentary distraction. One of the blue bolts grazed my shoulder, and my sleeve caught fire. I pounded it out with my free hand and risked a shot with my gun. Part of the gingerbread wall blew off. The witch screamed in rage. I risked a leap, knocking her to the floor. She writhed under my grip.

Before I could read her rights, the witch started to shrink, and I lost my grip on her. Suddenly, a rat ran out of her now-empty dress. The rodent raced through the candy door, screaming a spell as it exited. The wand, which had rolled under the work shelves when I tackled the witch, exploded into a million pieces, setting the whole room on fire. I slapped out my flaming shirt and grabbed the rope at my waist. I had to get out of that underground room before the fire reached those bottles full of chemicals. I pulled myself hand over hand through the misty doorway and scrambled blindly up the slide, unable to see anything except the flickering gray cliff with a vat of molasses pouring in the opposite direction. I couldn't have made it to the top without the rope.

It seemed like an eternity but was probably only a minute or two before the roof started lowering above me. I army-crawled out into the tunnel of the plastic Gingerbread House. I'd almost reached the final stretch when something in the witch's cottage detonated. The force of the explosion shot me out of the tunnel mouth and all the way across the room. I crashed into the platform inside Santa's grotto, and a Christmas tree dropped on my head. I lay stunned for a moment, but instinct screamed that another, bigger explosion was at hand. The witch's cottage had been full of strange chemicals. I got up on all fours and scrambled underneath the platform holding Santa's Chair, trailing by the severed rope, several strings of holiday garland, and the lower half of the plastic Christmas tree. A moment later, a second explosion blew the roof off the mall and brought the entire north wing crashing down around me.

The platform kept the worst of the debris off, but I was trapped underneath it. I'd have to wait for a rescue crew to dig me out. I kept thinking about the children. Had they made it out of the building in time? Had Mulligan brought them to safety, or were they trapped under the debris, like me?

I drifted in and out of consciousness, until I heard Mulligan's voice calling to me from somewhere above. I gasped a reply, coughing and choking from the dust in the air. A few minutes later, the rescue team lifted me out and strapped me to a stretcher.

"The kids! Did you get the kids?" I gasped.

"They are all safe, thanks to you," Mulligan said. "I got them out of the building just before the explosion. What happened down there?"

I gasped out as much of the story as I thought Mulligan would believe, about the underground room, the kids in cages, and a crazy woman in a witch's costume shooting at me. "She set the room on fire," I concluded. "It was full of chemicals, so that may be the source of the explosion. But she was crazy enough to have set off a bomb, for all I know. I just climbed out as fast as I could before I burned to death, and the explosion caught me just as I emerged from the Gingerbread House."

"I see that," Mulligan said. "The kids said she was threatening to eat them. She put them in cages and kept giving them candy to fatten them up. The six-year-old girl is really sharp. She told the boys not to eat the candy, just to eat bread and water so they wouldn't get fat. The kidnapper was really angry with her. I wonder if the woman made it out alive?"

"The crazy ones always do," I groaned as they loaded me into the ambulance.

"Talk about it later," said the EMT firmly, and shut the door in Mulligan's face.

The explosion destroyed the whole north wing of the mall and most of the evidence surrounding the kidnapping. A burnt wooden cage and some strange herbs were found among the debris in Santa's Workshop. They were presumed to have been blown out of the hidden room below. It was deemed enough evidence to verify the story told by myself and the children. The kidnapper was never found.

The newspapers called Mulligan and me heroes for saving the kidnapped children. I didn't like all the fuss. We were just doing our duty.

Sometimes, late at night, I think about the stranger parts of the case. The sense I had of going back in time, the view of an ancient forest through the window, the blue fire coming from the wand, the transformation from woman to rat that allowed the kidnapper to escape. I couldn't explain any of it and I didn't try. People would think I was insane. Only the rescued children and I knew the full truth.

25

See My Gray Foot Dangle

CHATTANOOGA, TENNESSEE

Her father stopped smiling when Mama died. Anna didn't realize it at first, so caught up was she with her own grief. But it was true. The happy grin he perpetually wore when working the forge or talking with friends or playing games with her was replaced with a grave twitch of the lips in the years following her mother's passing. He was a good father. She loved him as dearly as he loved her. But she missed his happy grin and belly laugh.

Anna was almost eleven when a new family arrived in their little town in the foothills. A young widow and her elderly mother came to live with their cousin, who worked at the local sawmill. Rumor said they fled from the old country due to politics. The widow, Sylvia, had hair so fair it was almost white, and her gentle eyes were green. Anna thought she must be a princess escaped from Fairy Land when she first saw the newcomer. The old woman was as gnarled and wiry as an old willow tree, and had a merry spirit and sharp tongue that made her a favorite with all the children in town. The same could not be said of the adults, who disliked the newcomers with their foreign accents, strange ways, and odd customs.

SEE MY GRAY FOOT DANGLE

Her father, hard at work at the smithy, barely noted the presence of the newcomers in town. Until one morning, when he came face to face with Sylvia on the wooden sidewalk in front of the Mercantile. He stopped so abruptly that eleven-year-old Anna bumped into him, and he stood with mouth agape, unable to speak a word, as Sylvia nodded graciously to him in passing. Anna exchanged glances with Sylvia's mother, who started cackling as soon as she saw the look on the blacksmith's rugged face. The women passed them in an instant and continued walking down the street. Father turned to look after them, a bemused smile on his face. Anna started to giggle and couldn't stop, especially when her father finally came to his senses and looked her way with a blush.

Sylvia took Anna to her heart as a daughter when she married Anna's father. She helped her with schoolwork, made lovely dresses for her, and taught her about herbs and wildcrafting. She also encouraged Anna's gift in the dairy. When Anna made cheeses, they tasted better than any others sold in the foothills.

Sylvia's mother also took Anna to her heart. Anna called her "Granny." She told her stories from the old country, tales of elves and trolls, witches and wizards, lords and ladies. And she hinted more than once that the old tales had meaning even here in the New World. She encouraged Anna to leave small gifts out for the spirits that guarded the house, the dairy, and the forge, and to honor those who guarded the forest and hills. But she also warned her against the supernatural beings who wished harm to the people who lived in the villages and towns.

"Trolls," she muttered at least once a week, when the bread failed to rise, spoons went missing, or someone stole their best laying hen. "I do not know the name for them in this place, but in the old country, we called them trolls. You be watchful, my Anna. They like to eat children even more than chickens."

"Mother, do not frighten my daughter," Sylvia said, patting Anna's shoulder as she sat with her schoolbooks at the kitchen table. "She is safe in this place. We put every protection around this house. All my children will be safe here." She patted her softly rounded belly with a proud smile and Anna grinned. Finally, she was going to have a younger sibling to love.

"That chicken was not safe," muttered Granny, but subsided when Sylvia gave her a stern look.

A few days later, a message came from Anna's uncle begging her father to come take over the forge in his mountain village, since a tragic accident had claimed the life of the previous blacksmith. The smithy came with a house, a barn, and several outbuildings: plenty of room for their growing family. Her father accepted the place immediately. The local villagers continued to treat Sylvia and her mother with coldness, despite her marriage to the local blacksmith. Anna's father wanted to live in a place where the whole family was accepted without remark. So they packed up their household and left within a week of receiving the letter.

As soon as Granny saw the crooked stone home that came with the smithy, tucked into a rocky corner of the mountain and backed by an old forest, she started cursing under her breath. Sylvia also stared at the house with a troubled frown. Anna's father, busy tying up the horses to the hitching post, missed their reaction. But Anna did not. "Trolls," muttered Granny. This time, Sylvia did not contradict her.

When Anna's uncle and his wife came to welcome them to their new home, they brought three tiny cousins with them. As

Anna tumbled about the yard with the children, Sylvia asked about the stone house. Uncle looked uncomfortable, and for good reason. The previous blacksmith had disappeared from the property a few weeks ago, and only a few grisly bits of him had been found, deep in the woods.

"But there's no need to worry," Anna's uncle hastened to say. "The local villages banded together and put on a hunt. We tracked and killed a large bear that lived near the peak. So, everyone is safe now."

"You are certain it was the bear that killed him?" pressed Granny, eyes narrow.

Uncle shrugged. "What else could it be?"

Anna could tell that Sylvia and Granny were not so sure. But they let the matter drop and turned their task to unpacking their wagons. Within an hour, every able-bodied person in their small village was bustling around the property, helping their family move into the house and forge. Anna's small herd of milk cows was led into the pasture beside a decaying old dairy, which the villagers promised to refurbish for her. The dairy building stood several hundred feet below the crooked stone house, not far from the edge of a cliff. The view from the dairy was spectacular, displaying row after row of blue mountains marching off into the distance. And the dropoff made fencing unnecessary on one side of the dairy pasture, which saved the family some money. From the chatter among the villagers assisting with the move-in, it was a toss-up who they were more excited to welcome into their village: the new blacksmith or his cheese-making daughter.

Granny cackled at the look on the blacksmith's face when he heard everyone exclaiming over Anna, and said: "People think with their stomachs, oft as not."

"I'm proud of our girl," he replied, grinning sheepishly in return.

Sylvia imposed one rule upon Anna when they moved into their new home. At the first sign of dusk, Anna was to return to the house where it was safe. There would be no roaming after dark on this mountain.

"But they killed the bear," Anna protested. In her home in the foothills, she was used to roaming at will wherever and whenever she chose.

But Sylvia was adamant, and Father backed her up, saying: "I do not care if you are grumpy, so long as you aren't dead." So that was that.

When the renovated dairy was ready for use, the twilight rule that Sylvia imposed was extended to include her work in the dairy. Anna must wrap up her cheesemaking and be inside the stone house before twilight fell. No lingering outside in the blue hour. No nighttime stargazing. The mountain was a dangerous place at night.

Anna was skeptical. What could be so dangerous that she couldn't go out at night? And why only her? Her father took evening strolls to the tavern and Granny went out after dark to harvest night-blooming mountain herbs. The restriction made no sense, but she abided by it since it brought Sylvia peace of mind. Still, she thought her new mother was overreacting to the death of the previous blacksmith. Hopefully, she would relax after the baby was born and things could go back to normal.

A few weeks after they opened the new dairy, Anna traded cheese cultures with a dairyman from the far side of the mountain. Excited by her new acquisition, she spent the whole day making a new cheese from the cultures. It was finicky work, and the process he recommended was just different enough from her usual method that it slowed her down considerably. She did not notice the light waning as she cut the curds repeatedly into smaller squares than normal. She did not notice the unnatural silence that seized the world outside the dairy. She ignored the heavy footsteps of something large stalking out of the woods, cruel eyes fixed on the dairy door.

Anna was hovering over the pot, waiting anxiously for the curds to settle so she could begin pressing them when the front door of the dairy banged open, and Sylvia swept inside with a lantern. Granny was not far behind, carrying a smoking bundle of herbs in her hands. Anna was startled by the combination of anger and fear on her new mother's face. Sylvia towered elegantly above her, like a Fairy Queen facing a recalcitrant subject.

Anna glanced desperately toward Granny to see if she would intercede for her, but the elderly woman remained on the doorstep, waving her burning herbs in the same ritual motions she'd used when she warded their stone house. A few yards up the hill, Anna glimpsed something large and menacing retreating toward the forest. She gasped, her heart pounding in sudden fear. Her legs folded abruptly, and she fell to the floor.

Tiny, pregnant Sylvia lifted Anna and her cheese pot into her arms as if they weighed nothing at all and marched to the dairy door. Anna had just enough presence of mind to grab her cheesecloth and weights as her mother swept past the table. Then the women were running up the hill toward the stone house as if it was their sole refuge from the monster Anna had glimpsed through the door.

Sylvia slammed inside and dropped Anna and her cheese pot onto the couch, gasping: "Do not *ever* disobey me in this matter! I could not bear to lose another. . . ." She stopped abruptly, clutching her belly as a sharp contraction caught her mid-sentence. She dropped into a kitchen chair, calling for Granny, who was waving her herbal smudge just outside the front door. Granny trotted inside and realized immediately what was going on.

"Finish your cheese and go to bed," Granny said sternly to Anna. "The babe will be here by morning."

Granny guided Sylvia into the room she shared with Anna's father and closed the door, leaving Anna to make her trembling way to the kitchen table with pot, weights, and cheesecloth. Shaking, unable to process what had just happened, Anna automatically scrubbed the table, washed her hands, and donned a new apron. When she was sure everything was clean, she consolidated the mass of curds in the pot, wrapped the mass in cheesecloth, and began pressing the new cheese to drain the whey. The familiarity of the task calmed her shaking hands and stilled her mind enough to think.

Something was stalking their property. Something big and frightening. Anna's legs trembled at the memory. Sylvia and Granny considered the . . . the thing to be more of a menace to her than to themselves. Or maybe they thought themselves more capable of fighting it than a young girl.

In any case, they had risked themselves to save her this evening, and now Sylvia was having her baby a month early. At the thought, Anna thrust the molded cheese under the pressing weights and ran to the slop bucket to be sick. What if Sylvia died? What if the baby died? It would be her fault for being defiant and staying too long in the dairy.

At that moment, her father came wearily in the door. Anna wiped her mouth, straightened her dress, and went to tell him what happened. She feared what he would say about her disobedience and its dire consequences. To her surprise, Father just hugged her fiercely, told her to listen to her mama from now on, and then whispered the reassurances she needed to hear. That mother and baby would be fine. That he loved her very much. That she was more important than a new cheese, and she'd better remember that from now on. After extracting a promise of obedience from her, Father sent Anna to bed with a loaf of bread and went to check on his wife.

In the morning, Anna had a baby sister to cherish. When Granny placed the child in Anna's arms, she was amazed at how sturdy the tiny girl was. She was as fair as Sylvia and her ears came to points. Or did they? Granny quickly adjusted the blanket, and when she stepped away, the baby's ears were normal. They named her Rosa, and Anna adored her at once. While Sylvia, weakened from childbirth, lay abed recovering her strength, Anna carried the baby everywhere with her: to the shops, to gather herbs with Granny, to visit her small cousins, to the dairy to make the new cheese, which had proved so popular she could not keep up with the demand. Sylvia laughingly complained that she didn't get to spend enough time with her two girls. "I only see you for meals," she teased.

Once she had recovered, Sylvia started dropping by the dairy at sunset to help Anna finish her tasks and walk her home. If she went out on a late errand to the village, Granny would accompany her. When Anna watched the small cousins for her uncle and aunt, her father would stop by to pick her up and drive her home in the wagon. None of them explained why. They didn't need to. Just the thought of the monster she'd seen the night Rosa was born was enough to trigger the nightmares Anna had suffered since her sister's birth.

"Granny, what was that thing?" Anna whispered once when they were alone together in the kitchen preparing dinner.

Granny made a gesture to ward off evil and replied: "Night troll." And refused to say another word.

Winter came early to their mountain village. The first snow fell in October, and by the middle of November, Anna's little cousins could talk about nothing but Christmas. Would they celebrate Baby Jesus's birthday? Would Saint Nicholas give them presents? Would they have a feast? They made a list of presents they hoped to receive, and Anna memorized it. Their wants were so small. A doll. A sled. A toy soldier. And stockings. They wanted lots and lots of stockings.

Sylvia chuckled when she heard their list. "We will cover the toys, if you will knit stockings," she said to Anna. "We will have the whole family come over on Christmas Day to open presents, and then we will feast and feast and feast!"

Anna laughed and agreed. She went to the village shop to purchase yarn for the stockings. The shopkeeper and his wife were delighted when she told them about her Christmas present for the little cousins, and the shopkeeper promised to buy yarn in many bright colors when he next went to town.

Between minding the baby, making cheese, attending school, and knitting stockings, Anna was busy every moment of the day. But it was a happy bustle, and she was pleased with her new life on the mountain. Especially now that she knew that

Sylvia's fears were not misplaced. She did not want her little cousins or Rosa to fall victim to the menacing figure that still stalked her dreams. So she watched over the children carefully and made sure everyone was safely inside by dark.

To give her aunt time to hand-make Christmas presents for the children, Anna started bringing her little cousins back to her house after school. They would have a snack and do their schoolwork around the kitchen table, while Granny bustled about preparing herbal remedies or starting dinner preparations. Over milk and cookies, Granny would tell the children stories about the Yule Lads who used to visit her village in the old country.

"I remember those troll lads," Granny said, pouring milk into their cups. "The sons of old Gryla the giantess and her lazy husband. Those Yule Lads were silly pranksters, who made mischief for children who weren't well-behaved and didn't do their chores. Starting December 12, you had to be good, or the Yule Lads would play tricks on you."

"Meat Scraper, Skye Gobbler, Spoon Licker, Pot Scraper," chanted little Karl, holding out his plate for more cookies.

"Gully Gawk, Door Slammer, Window Peeper, Sausage Swiper," listed Evie, not to be outdone by her younger sibling.

"Such naughty trolls," Granny said. "If you ever come across a troll, don't look at it. Don't invite it in."

"But they don't live here," little Friedrich said sadly. "No trolls come to our village."

Anna looked at Granny sharply. Their eyes met for a moment, then Granny calmly misdirected their young audience, saying: "No Yule Lads here. You will have to make each other behave."

Anna laughed and said: "Evie can be Spoon Licker; Karl can be Door Slammer; and Friedrich can be Pot Scraper."

The three little cousins perked up at this fanciful notion and started listing alternatives: "Tree climber. Nose picker. Cookie swiper."

"Home goer," Anna called at last, her sides sore from laughing. The day was growing short, and they all needed to be home before dark. She hustled them into their cloaks and walked them to her uncle's house. They were gabbling excitedly to their mother about the Yule Lads and their new nicknames when Anna turned for home.

Granny was still at work in the kitchen when Anna returned. She put on an apron and started chopping vegetables. Once her hands were busy, she asked: "What should you do, Granny, if a troll comes to your home?" In case of an emergency, Anna did not want to feel as helpless as she had the night Sylvia rescued her from the troll.

"Smudge the air with protective herbs," Granny said, motioning to the bundles drying around them. "If it sings to you, then sing back."

She proceeded to give Anna her first lesson on trolls. After that, whenever Anna and Granny were alone, they spoke of troll lore and how to protect yourself from the stone giants who liked human flesh to eat, and sometimes stole children from their beds.

Calamity, they say, comes in threes. The first sign of trouble came the week before Christmas, when a letter arrived saying her aunt's mother was deathly ill. The letter begged for her aunt and uncle to come at once. So the little ones were bundled up and brought to Anna's house to stay in her care until their parents' return.

"Will Grandmother die?" little Evie whispered to Anna.

"I don't know," she said sadly. "Maybe."

"Will Saint Nicholas know where we've gone?"

"Oh yes," Anna replied more confidently. "I am sure he knows you are staying here. He will leave presents for you on Christmas Eve."

Anna picked her up and hugged her tight. Then she sent her to play with her brothers and baby Rosa.

It was a full house that evening and the little cousins got into everything. Sylvia loaded all their Christmas gifts into two big baskets and asked Anna to hide them in the dairy until Christmas Eve.

"I feel like Saint Nicholas in reverse," Anna joked, sneaking out the back door while Granny distracted the little cousins with cookies and another tale of the Yule Lads.

The children were as good as it was possible to be for active youngsters in the week before Christmas. Anna and her father took them sledding several times on the far side of the village, since the hill behind their home was too dangerous because of the cliff. This gave Sylvia and Granny time to cook and clean and prepare for the holiday feast.

Two days before Christmas, baby Rosa woke in the night with a high fever. None of Granny's remedies could bring it down, so Anna's father loaded Sylvia and the baby into a sleigh and drove down the steep mountain track to the town in the foothills where the doctor lived, leaving the little cousins in Granny and Anna's care.

With Christmas Eve came the snow. It started with a few flakes in the morning, but conditions worsened in the afternoon. "I will milk the cows and get the Christmas gifts from the dairy, before we are snowed in," Anna said to Granny as the short afternoon drew to a close. She pulled on her cloak and thrust her feet into snowshoes to help her stay above the drifts.

Just before she went through the door, Granny shoved a parcel into Anna's arms. "You will need this, in case the Night Troll returns," she said grimly. "Twilight comes early during a storm." Anna nodded and hugged the bundle close as she hurried downhill through the heavy wet snow.

The milking was soon done, and Anna settled the cattle in for the night before carrying the heavy pails to the dairy. The dairy door was covered with ice and hard to open. Anna had to shove repeatedly before she could get inside. The building itself was frigid. The windows had no glass in them, and snow had blown right through the gaps in the shutters. Stepping through the drifts on the floor, Anna deposited the last two pails of milk and shivered her way into the storeroom where the cheeses were aging. The two baskets of presents were right where she'd hidden them. She was bending to pick them up when a happy shout echoed through the main cheesemaking room. Anna whirled and hurried through the door. Three red-cheeked faces beamed at her from under snow-laden hoods. "We followed you! We found you!" the little cousins cheered. "We are good trackers," little Karl boasted.

"You are supposed to be up at the house," Anna said. "You know the rule. You need to be home by twilight."

"But you went outside," Evie said.

"I'm doing the farm chores," Anna said. "Milking the cows and storing the milk in the dairy."

Anna glanced uneasily through the door into the snowstorm. Darkness was falling even faster than the snow. "Wait right here! I need to pick up some . . . cheese for our Christmas feast. Then we will run as fast as we can up the hill to Granny. First one there wins the game."

As the little cousins cheered, Anna returned to the storeroom, tossed several cloth-wrapped cheeses into the two baskets of presents, and then hustled the little ones back out the door. Worry made her careless with her steps. Anna shoved the door shut with no thought of the ice beneath her feet, and then slipped and toppled down the steps, her ankle twisting badly beneath her. The pain was instant, and agonizing. The little cousins were already running up the long slope toward the house, cheering each other on. But Karl and Evie heard Anna's cry of pain and turned around. Seeing her lying on the ground, they ran back to see what was wrong.

Anna knew she couldn't walk. Just lying still was agony. But if she stayed where she was, she would freeze to death long before any troll could come for her. She had to move. Evie and Karl helped her sit up, which made her head swim. She swayed and vomited sideways into the snow, trying to avoid the gift baskets that were still looped around her arms.

Faintly, through the dizziness, she heard Friedrich shouting happily for Granny to open the door to the stone house, for he had won the race. A moment later, she heard Granny calling anxiously for the other children. Anna knew she should send them home quickly, before full dark brought the night troll to their door.

But it was too late. Over the anxious questions of her two little cousins, Anna heard the same giant footsteps that she'd ignored the night Sylvia rescued her. Something was coming toward them, shaking the trees at the edge of the forest. Something huge.

"We must get in the dairy. Right now," Anna said through chattering teeth. "Help me! Quickly, cousins."

The cousins picked up immediately on her fear. Supporting her on either side, they helped her back up the stairs. Anna leaned against the wall as they forced the ice-laden door open. She hobbled through and her leg gave way. As she fell, she shrieked for the children to close and bar the door.

Anna blacked out briefly, but the slamming of the dairy door awakened her. Karl and Evie were struggling with the heavy bar, as she sat up, trying to control her stomach. She did not want to vomit again. She tried to think through the agonizing pain. Barring the door was a good start, but that alone would not keep them safe through the long winter night. The window shutters were easily broken by the troll, and winter cold could freeze them to death if they did not have enough wood to sustain a fire through the night.

Anna's thoughts were interrupted by her little cousins, who turned to face her after barring the dairy door.

"Saint Nicholas was here," breathed Evie.

Anna blinked in surprise. Then she realized that she had dropped the two baskets full of Christmas gifts when she blacked out. Their contents had scattered across the floor when she blacked out, and brightly wrapped presents were strewn everywhere.

"Saint Nicholas saw us in the dairy and thought he should deliver his gifts here," agreed Karl. "We aren't supposed to see him, so he dropped the presents on the floor when we came back too soon."

In spite of their dire situation, Anna had to smile. The children had come up with a much better explanation than any she could have contrived. Still, they had to make themselves secure first, and then she could figure out what to do about the Christmas gifts.

Anna said: "We need to warm up the dairy before we open presents. And we need to wrap my injured ankle."

Recalled to their task, the children helped Anna into a chair and followed her instructions, lighting the fire, piling enough wood beside it so Anna could feed it during the night, and wrapping cheesecloth around her ankle as tightly as they could.

Then Anna unpacked a bundle of herbs Granny had given her and crumbled some of them over the flames as a smudge to keep the troll at bay. There weren't enough herbs to last the whole night, she realized with a sinking heart. But there was no need to frighten the children, so she said nothing about it. Instead, she made a game of their situation, telling the children they would have a Christmas sleepover in the dairy. She bade them gather the scattered gifts and organize them into piles for each person. Then they pulled out the snacks Anna kept on hand in the dairy and toasted cheese over bread for their dinner while the winter storm raged around them. Then Anna had them set up their beds with blankets and old straw from the lean-to attached to the dairy.

Anna heard the massive footsteps once again as they made themselves comfortable around the fire. The thuds grew louder, and she knew the troll was walking toward the barn. Evie looked up with a frown. "What is that sound, Anna?" she asked. "Is Granny coming to fetch us?"

"It is just the storm playing with a shutter," Anna fibbed. A blizzard wind obligingly shook the small dairy, as if it wanted to confirm her story. "Granny is up at the house, watching Friedrich." Anna forced herself to speak calmly, though her heart slammed painfully against her ribs. "We will see her in the morning when the blizzard stops." To distract them from the troll, she added: "I think we should each open one present to celebrate Christmas Eve before we go to sleep."

Karl and Evie cheered and forgot all about the loud footsteps, which had halted near the window behind Anna's worktable. They spent quite some time fingering each present before making their choice. Strangely enough, they both chose the package of stockings Anna had knit for each of them. They each opened their gift and exclaimed excitedly over the brightly colored stockings that toppled forth. The stockings were each tried on, and much hilarity ensued. Karl hopped across the workroom in his red socks, crying: "See my red foot hop! Hop, hop, hop." Not to be outdone, Evie donned her yellow pair and said: "See my yellow foot dance. Dance, Dance, Dance."

Through the window, a gravelly voice whispered: "See my gray foot dangle. Dangle, Dangle, Dangle."

Anna gasped with fear, but the laughing children had not heard. She dropped more herbs on the fire and heard the night troll retreat toward the edge of the cliff. When it was gone, she called the children to order and sang them lullabies until they went to sleep.

At midnight, she was wakened from a doze by a gravelly voice crooning from the window: "There's a pretty little hand, daughter dear, and lullaby." There was enchantment in the song, and it sizzled along Anna's skin, making her hands twitch. She wanted to walk around the worktable and open the shutters for the owner of the voice. Remembering Granny's troll lessons, Anna responded: "In filth it has never been found, hellsprite, my Kari and hushaby." So saying, she sprinkled more herbs on the fire. The voice grumbled and backed away from the dairy.

At 2:00 a.m., the gravelly voice came again: "There's a pretty little eye, daughter dear, and lullaby." The enchantment tugged at Anna's heart, bidding her turn around and look into the eyes of the singer. Anna thrust a bunch of herbs under her nose and replied: "Never did it evil spy, hellsprite, my Kari and hushaby." She sprinkled more herbs on the fire, but carefully now, for she was running low. The troll cursed and withdrew to the cliff's edge.

At 4:00 a.m., the troll returned. "There's a pretty little foot, daughter dear, and lullaby," the gravelly voice crooned. The song made Anna's feet twitch. It took all of Anna's waning strength to resist the enchantment bidding her to walk toward the troll. Whispering a prayer, Anna said: "Never did it trample dirt, hellsprite, my Kari and hushaby."

Anna had only a handful of herbs left. She sprinkled half on the fire. The voice swore and stepped back, but it did not retreat. Anna hugged her shawl tightly around her, feeling desperate. She must protect her sleeping cousins, but she did not have enough of the smudge left to drive the night troll away from the dairy.

Placing another log on the fire, she softly sang Christmas carols to drown out the voice of the night troll. The holy words angered the voice at the window. It muttered and cursed, and finally the troll retreated to the edge of the cliff.

Just before dawn, the blizzard ceased. The sky was lightening toward day when heavy footsteps approached the dairy. The voice came once more at the window. "Day begins to dawn, daughter dear, and lullaby," the gravelly voice crooned. Anna jerked awake and threw the last of the herbs on the fire. Sitting up straight, she commanded: "Stand and turn to stone, hellsprite, my Kari and hushaby." Withdrawing a knife from her granny's packet, she threw it at the window. The runes on the blade flashed brightly as it embedded itself into the wooden shutter barring the window where the night troll crouched. Cursing, the troll backed away from the dairy. Suddenly, the sun crested the eastern horizon, turning the gray dawn into the dazzling whiteness of new fallen snow. The entire world held its breath as sunlight swept over troll, dairy, barn, and cow pasture. For a moment, there was no sound save the wind.

Then Anna heard Granny's voice bellowing from the stone house: "Anna! Anna! Anna!" And she knew it was safe. She had triumphed over the night troll.

The night after Christmas, the blacksmith's family reunited around the holiday table to eat their delayed feast. The baby's fever had broken on Christmas Day and Rosa was recovering quickly. A letter had arrived that morning, Anna's aunt explaining that her mother had turned the corner and was expected to live. And Granny had examined Anna's ankle and declared that it was sprained, not broken, so she too was on the mend.

It was a nine-days wonder in the village when the locals discovered that an enormous rock had suddenly appeared on the edge of the cliff behind the dairy. Where had it come from? There was no rocky outcropping above it to explain its sudden presence, and no avalanche or rockfall disturbed the surrounding hillside. How could such a massive boulder have appeared in a such a prominent place with no sign of its passing? Speculation was rampant, yet no one remarked upon the fact that the stone looked exactly like a giant turned to stone.

Anna and her family agreed that it was a mystery but declined further comment. For what else could they say? No one in the village would believe the true story.

Resources

Asala, Joanne. *Norwegian Troll Tales.* Iowa City, IA: Penfield Books, 1994.

Asfar, Daniel. *Ghost Stories of America.* Edmonton, AB: Ghost House Books, 2001.

Bader, Chris. *Strange Northwest.* Blaine, WA: Hancock House, 1995.

Battle, Kemp P. *Great American Folklore.* New York: Doubleday, 1986.

Botkin, B. A., ed. *New York City Folklore.* New York: Random House, 1956.

———. *A Treasury of American Folklore.* New York: Crown, 1944.

Boucher, Alan. *Elves, Trolls and Elemental Beings: Icelandic Folktales II.* Reykjavik, Iceland: Icelandic Review Library, 1981,

Briggs, Jonathan. *Urban Mythletoe—the Story of the Mistletoe Bride.* Mistletoediary.com. Accessed 6/13/2022, https://mistletoediary.com/2012/12/04/urban-mythletoe-the-story-of-the-mistletoe-bride/.

Brown, D. *Legends.* Eugene: Randall V. Mills Archive of Northwest Folklore at the University of Oregon, 1971.

Brunvand, Jan Harold. *The Choking Doberman and Other Urban Legends.* New York: W. W. Norton, 1984.

———. *The Vanishing Hitchhiker.* New York: W. W. Norton, 1981.

Cherrell, Kate. *The Bramshill House Bride, or the Legend of the Mistletoe Bough.* Burialsandbeyond.com. Accessed 6/13/2022, https://burialsandbeyond.com/2019/12/21/the-bramshill-house-bride-or-the-legend-of-the-mistletoe-bough/.

Christensen, Jo-Anne. *Ghost Stories of Christmas.* Edmonton, AB: Lone Pine Publishing, 2001.

———. *Haunted Christmas.* Edmonton, AB: Ghost House Books, 2002.

Coffin, Tristram P., and Hennig Cohen, eds. *Folklore from the Working Folk of America.* New York: Doubleday, 1973.

————*Folklore in America*. New York: Doubleday & AMP, 1966.

Cohen, Daniel. *Ghostly Tales of Love & Revenge*. New York: Putnam, 1992.

Cohen, Daniel, and Susan Cohen. *Hauntings & Horrors*. New York: Dutton Children's Books, 2002.

Crain, Mary Beth. *Haunted Christmas: Yuletide Ghosts and Other Spooky Holiday Happenings*. Guilford, CT: Globe Pequot Press, 2010.

Curtiss, Phebe A. *Christmas Stories and Legends*. Columbia, SC: Timeless Classic Books, 2010.

Davis, Jefferson. *Ghosts and Strange Critters of Washington and Oregon*. Vancouver, WA: Norseman Ventures, 1999.

dePaola, Tomie. *The Legend of the Poinsettia*. New York: Penguin Putnam Books for Young Readers, 1994.

Dewhurst, C. Kurt, and Yvonne R. Lockwood, eds. *Michigan Folklife Reader*. East Lansing: Michigan State University Press, 1988.

Dobie, J. Frank, ed. *Legends of Texas*. Austin: Texas Folklore Society, 1924.

————. *Tone the Bell Easy*. Dallas, TX: Southern Methodist University Press, 1932.

Dorson, R. M. *America in Legend*. New York: Pantheon, 1973.

Downer, Deborah L., ed. *Classic American Ghost Stories*. Little Rock, AR: August House, 2005.

"Dr. Funk Tells Some Ghost Stories. Remarkable Narratives of Actual Occurrences by a Clergy-man of Renown." *Trenton (NJ) Sunday Advertiser*, November 19, 1905.

Dunham, Terri Hoover. *The Legend of Papa Noel: A Cajun Christmas Story*. Ann Arbor, MI: Sleeping Bear Press, 2006.

Editors of Life. *The Life Treasury of American Folklore*. New York: Time Inc., 1961.

Flanagan, J. T., and A. P. Hudson. *The American Folk Reader*. New York: A. S. Barnes, 1958.

Gatschet, Albert S. "Oregonian Folk-Lore." *Journal of American Folklore*, Vol. 4, No. 13, 1891, 139–43. DOI: 10,2307/533930.

Resources

Gethard, Chris. *Weird New York*. New York: Sterling, 2005.

Godfrey, Linda S. *Weird Michigan*. New York: Sterling, 2006.

Hauck, Dennis William. *Haunted Places: The National Directory*. New York: Penguin Books, 1994.

"A Haunted House. The Wild, Weird Antics of an Animated Skeleton." *Cleveland Plain Dealer*, March 10, 1889.

Helm, Mike. *Oregon's Ghosts and Monsters*. Eugene, OR: Rainy Day Press, 1983.

Herman, Heidi. *The Legend of the Icelandic Yule Lads*. Denver: Outskirts Press, 2015.

Herrick, Bertha F. *Myths and Legends of Christmas Tide*. San Francisco: Stanley-Taylor Company, 1901.

Holub, Joan. *The Haunted States of America*. New York: Aladdin Paperbacks, 2001.

Jagendorf, M. A. *The Ghost of Peg-Leg Peter and Other Stories of Old New York*. New York: Vanguard Press, 1965.

Jerman, Tom A. *Santa Claus Worldwide: A History of St. Nicholas and Other Holiday Gift-Bringers*. Jefferson, NC: McFarland, 2020.

Jones, Louis C. *Things That Go Bump in the Night*. New York: Hill and Wang, 1959.

Jones, Suzi. *Oregon Folklore*. Eugene: University of Oregon and the Oregon Arts Commission, 1977.

Kellermeyer, M. Grant, M.A., ed. *Fireside Ghost Stories for Christmas Eve: An Anthology of Winter Horror Tales*. Fort Wayne, IN: Oldstyle Tales Press, 2015.

Kirk, Tanya, ed. *Spirits of the Season: Christmas Hauntings*. London, England: British Library, 2018.

Lamb, John J. *San Diego Specters*. San Diego: Sunbelt Publications, 1999.

Leach, M. *The Rainbow Book of American Folk Tales and Legends*. New York: World Publishing, 1958.

Leary, James P. *Wisconsin Folklore*. Madison: University of Wisconsin Press, 1998.

229

Leeming, David, and Jake Pagey. *Myths, Legends, & Folktales of America*. New York: Oxford University Press, 1999.

Marinacci, Mark. *Mysterious California*. Los Angeles: Panpipes Press, 1988.

"A Maritime Ghost." *Cincinnati Daily Enquirer*, September 12, 1869.

"A Milk White Ghost. And the Consternation Which It Created on Shipboard." *Cleveland Plain Dealer*, May 12, 1895.

Moore, Tara, ed. *The Valancourt Book of Victorian Christmas Ghost Stories*. Richmond, VA: Valancourt Books, 2016.

Mott, A. S. *Ghost Stories of America, Volume II*. Edmonton, AB: Ghost House Books, 2003.

———. *Ghost Stories of Wisconsin*. Auburn, WI: Lone Pine Publishing International, 2006.

Norman, Michael. *Haunted Wisconsin, 3rd ed.*. Madison, WI: Terrace Books, 2011.

Norman, Michael, and Beth Scott. *Haunted Heartland*. New York: Warner Books, 1985.

———. *Historic Haunted America*. New York: Tor Books, 1995.

Okonowicz, Ed. *The Big Book of Maryland Ghost Stories*. Mechanicsburg, PA: Stackpole, 2010.

Peck, Catherine, ed. *A Treasury of North American Folk Tales*. New York: W. W. Norton, 1998.

Pohlen, Jerome. *Oddball Wisconsin*. Chicago: Chicago Review Press, 2001.

Polley, J., ed. *American Folklore and Legend*. New York: Reader's Digest Association, 1978.

Raedisch, Linda. *The Old Magic of Christmas: Yuletide Traditions for the Darkest Days of the Year*. Woodbury, MN: Llewellyn Publications, 2013.

Ridenour, Al. *The Krampus and the Old, Dark Christmas: Roots and Rebirth of the Folkloric Devil*. Port Townsend, WA: Feral House, 2016.

Roberts, Nancy. *Civil War Ghost Stories & Legends*. Columbia: University of South Carolina Press, 1992.

———. *The Haunted South*. Columbia: University of South Carolina Press, 1988.

Rule, Leslie. *Coast to Coast Ghosts*. Kansas City, MO: Andrews McMeel, 2001.

Schwartz, Alvin. *Scary Stories to Tell in the Dark*. New York: Harper Collins, 1981.

Simmons, William P., ed. *Yuletide Frights: Victorian Ghost Stories for Christmas*. New York: Shadow House Publishing, 2020.

Skinner, Charles M. *American Myths and Legends, Vol. 1*. Philadelphia: J. B. Lippincott, 1903.

———. *Myths and Legends of Our Own Land, Vol. 1 & 2*. Philadelphia: J. B. Lippincott, 1896.

Smith, Barbara. *Ghost Stories of California*. Renton, WA: Lone Pine, 2000.

Stansfield Jr, Charles A. *Haunted Ohio: Ghosts and Strange Phenomena of the Buckeye State*. Mechanicsburg, PA: Stackpole, 2008.

Thay, Edrick. *Ghost Stories of Ohio*. Edmonton, AB: Ghost House Books, 2001.

"The Ghost's Touch: A Christmas Story." *Indiana State Journal*, December 21, 1898.

"Three Warnings." *Ashtabula (OH) Weekly Telegraph*, May 15, 1869.

Treat, Wesley, Heather Shade, and Rob Riggs. *Weird Texas*. New York: Sterling, 2005.

Undine. *The Haunted Christmas Quilt*. Mountain View, CA: Strange Company, 2018. Accessed 10/9/21, http://strangeco.blogspot.com/2018/12/the-haunted-christmas-quilt.html.

Williams, Scott. *Haunted Texas*. Guilford, CT: Globe Pequot Press, 2007.

Willis, James A. *The Big Book of Ohio Ghost Stories*. Mechanicsburg, PA: Stackpole, 2013.

Wyman, Walker D. *Wisconsin Folklore*. River Falls: University of Wisconsin Press, 1979.

Young, Richard, and Judy Dockrey. *Ghost Stories from the American Southwest*. Little Rock, AR: August House, 1991.

Zeitlin, Steven J., Amy J. Kotkin, and Holly Cutting Baker. *A Celebration of American Family Folklore*. New York: Pantheon, 1982.

About the Author

Author S. E. Schlosser has been telling stories since she was a child, when games of "let's pretend" quickly built themselves into full-length stories. A graduate of the Institute of Children's Literature and Rutgers University, she also created and maintains the website

www.AmericanFolklore.net, where she shares a wealth of stories from all fifty states, some dating from the origins of America.

About the Illustrator

Artist Paul Hoffman trained in painting and printmaking. His first extensive illustration work on assignment was in Egypt, drawing ancient wall reliefs for the University of Chicago. His work graces books of many genres—including children's titles, textbooks, short story collections, natural history volumes, and numerous cookbooks. For *Spooky Christmas*, he employed a scratchboard technique and an active imagination.